The Tragedy of
APARTHEID

The Tragedy of
APARTHEID

A Journalist's Experiences in the South African Riots

by NORMAN PHILLIPS

DAVID McKAY COMPANY, INC.

New York

CONTENTS

ILLUSTRATIONS

following page 26

The Tragedy of
APARTHEID

APARTHEID

(*Song of the* c.o.p.*)

O, Apartheid brings us sorrow,
And Apartheid wrecks our lives,
And Apartheid kills our children,
And drives away our wives;
And we must carry passes,
In our country we're not free,
But the Congress of the People paves the road to liberty.

* The Congress of the People, including the African National Congress, the South African Indian Congress, the National Union of the Organization of Colored People, and the Congress of Democrats.

1. SHARPEVILLE

ON MONDAY MARCH 21, 1960, the first wave of black nationalism, sweeping southward through the African continent lapped against the fortress of Apartheid.

By nightfall sixty-seven Africans lay dead and 186 others nursed bullet-wounded bodies. They were the victims in the first of the new clashes of colour—shot down without warning by the South African police.

This was the Sharpeville massacre that made South Africa a pariah among nations. For a dozen years successive Nationalist governments of that country had been heading pell-mell for such a disaster. Obstinately committed to the doctrine of white supremacy, they failed to see that their harshly applied segregation policies were breeding hatred and hastening the inevitable tragedy.

"The events of 1960," said the Johannesburg *Sunday Times*, "were confidently expected only in 1980 at the earliest. But they are here with us now."

The irresistible force of African nationalism was in full collision with the implacable structure of Apartheid. For three uncertain weeks the two grappled with each other until the Africans, shorn of their leaders, retreated into sullen submission. A battle had been lost but the war had just begun.

Sharpeville, where it all began, is about thirty miles south of Johannesburg, but few of the big city's 1,052,600 residents could find it on a map. This is because Sharpeville is not only a comparatively new centre, but it is also a "native location," a suburb restricted to Africans. To get there, it is necessary to ask for directions to Vereeniging, the white industrial town that draws its labour from Sharpeville's 15,000 residents.

Vereeniging's previous claim to fame was as the site of the peace conference in 1902 ending the South African War. Its wide streets and square layout give it the appearance of a prairie town; but it is a factory city with its own power station, steel works, and industries, in addition to neighbouring coal mines.

Monday, March 21, the first day of the South African autumn, Vereeniging was unnaturally quiet. Only a few Africans were to be seen. The white butcher was reduced to delivering his own orders—a task normally relegated to Negro help. Other shopkeepers took brooms in unaccustomed hands and swept out their premises. White housewives, whose African help did not live in, made their own beds and prepared meals.

The Africans who dig Vereeniging's ditches, clean its streets and houses, and provide the factories with unskilled labour had stayed at home in Sharpeville. The buses that carry them the two miles to work ran empty and then stopped running.

For the previous ten days Sharpeville had been stirring uneasily. Although this was no shanty town but rather one of the better locations planned and built by the Government, its people were complaining of high rents, low wages, and unemployment. Most of the residents were living close to or below the bread-line level. A family of ten—and there were many of that size—could afford to send only three children to school. A family with five youngsters would be lucky if two got schooling. Infant mortality was high, and most of the graves in the location cemetery were occupied by child victims of gastro-enteritis and pneumonia.

In Sharpeville, as in other urban South African areas, a Negro can look forward to a life expectancy of thirty-eight years. Only fifty-five out of every hundred Negroes there reach the age of sixteen.

At mid-March the Anglican curate had reported to his superior in Johannesburg, Bishop Ambrose Reeves, that Sharpeville's misery was nearing the point of tension. This was no racial problem but a simple matter of economics— wages held down by government and industry, unemployment, comparatively high rents, and food costs in relation to wages. The price of food knew no colour bar. Black people paid the same price for groceries as white people. Black people ate less.

One more burden oppressed the people of Sharpeville. The laws of Apartheid demanded that from the age of sixteen, each man and woman carry a pass. The pass or reference book was required to work, to travel, and to live anywhere outside a jail. It was a document carrying the bearer's photograph, name, tax receipts, and record of employment.

Failure to produce a reference book on the demand of the police or an authorized member of the public was a criminal offence, with the usual fine $14 or five weeks imprisonment. And half a million of South Africa's nearly ten million Negroes are charged with offences against the pass laws each year.

No other law imposed by Apartheid has brought as much suffering and humiliation to the African as the pass laws.

They are the keystone of the white-supremacy structure to "keep the Kaffir in his place." Africans have two names for their reference books—the *verdomde* or *dompass* (the accursed pass), or simply the "badge of slavery."

Protests against the pass laws have gone on for many years; but Sharpeville happened to be chosen for a new type of demonstration by a newly organized group—the Pan-Africanist Congress. Led by a thirty-two-year-old university lecturer, Robert Mangaliso Sobukwe, the Pan-Africanists were angry young men who broke away from the established African National Congress to demand abolition of passes and full political rights by 1963.

The Pan-Africanists chose their name because they look to the newly independent nations of Africa for inspiration and help. Where the African National Congress dreams of a multi-racial society in South Africa, the Pan-Africanists plan for a black South Africa.

Sharpeville's hungry and impoverished people listened to the Pan-Africanists and they liked what they heard: "We will call you into action, and from that day onwards you will never carry a pass again."

The call to action was set for March 21. The plan was to march on police stations without passes, and to demand to be arrested. If the campaign was successful the jails and courts would overflow, and the factories and farms would be without their Negro labour.

Sergeant J. L. Grobler, who commanded the South African police detachment at Sharpeville, was not slow to notice the mounting tension within the location. He reported to Captain E. G. Cawood at the Vereeniging police station and on Friday evening, March 18, Cawood went out to Sharpeville where he was shown sixteen or seventeen pass books that had been defaced and discarded. This was an angry omen —for an African to throw away his pass was to give up his Apartheid-granted right to work.

Sunday brought more ominous signs. Late that night Cawood called out ten white and twenty-seven non-white policemen and again went into Sharpeville. Reports had reached them that groups of one hundred, three hundred, and five hundred Africans were roaming the location.

Cawood led his reinforcements to the police station. Some Africans were there, complaining of being assaulted and of having had their pass books seized by bands of Negroes who were moving through the suburb. The captain and his men went in search of the marauding bands. He met one group of Africans, young men between eighteen and twenty-four, some of whom were armed with sticks and some not. Cawood came to the conclusion that those without weapons were being detained by the others. There was a scuffle when he ordered his constables to disarm and disperse the band.

Rifle at the ready, Cawood continued his patrol. Shortly after midnight he encountered another band of Africans. This time the captain fired two shots into the ground as a warning, and the Africans vanished into the night. At 2 A.M. he encountered more Negroes apparently holding a meeting. Cawood ordered a baton charge to break up the gathering. In the course of the night he encountered about fifteen similar parties of Africans.

Sharpeville was seething. The police explanation was that a not-so-small number of bad Africans was intimidating the mass of law-abiding, good Africans. "It was my impression," said Cawood, "that the groups tried to chase all the native men from their homes."

The police and government version was a little too pat. No doubt there was intimidation as the Pan-Africanists drummed up support for Monday's protest, but the suggestion that terrorist bands held the majority of Sharpeville residents in thrall is hardly credible.

There was not a soul in Sharpeville without a grievance. Many may have been cowed into submission by fear of the police, but many more were ready for the call of the Pan-Africanists. Nor should it be considered surprising that in an African community where political action is still at a primitive level, there should be threats as to what might happen to a man who went to work on the day chosen for a strike and demonstration.

One other aspect of life in Sharpeville does bolster the police theory. Like any other South African Negro urban community, the location had its *tsotsis,* or Negro gangsters. They were a by-product of the Apartheid system, drawing their members from the youngsters without schools and the young men without jobs. It was easier for them to rob and prey upon their fellow Africans than to earn an honest living; and if there was to be violence, the lawless *tsotsis* would have a hand in it. Yet no one deplored their existence and tactics more than the Pan-Africanists, who were dedicated to Gandhi's philosophy of non-violent civil disobedience.

There was little sleep for anyone in Sharpeville Sunday night. At 5 A.M. Monday, before the dawn broke, a crowd of men, women, and children began gathering at the entrance to the location, where the buses waited to take workers down the dusty road to their jobs in Vereeniging. The crowd was determined no one should go to work that day.

The entrance to Sharpeville was marked by a chain stretched across the road, guarded by African policemen.

Outside the barrier there were several buildings housing the staff of the location's white administrator. By 7 A.M., Captain Cawood estimated that seven thousand people were massed at the barrier. He sent into Vereeniging for ten tear-gas bombs.

An African crowd taunting armed police is a fantastic spectacle. Cawood described the core of the demonstration as five hundred to six hundred young men marching up and down blowing whistles. There was more to it than that. The music of the whistles was a haunting, moving song of Africa. It set the crowd shuffling slowly forward, and then retreating.

Cawood ordered five tear-gas bombs to be fired. The crowd fell back about thirty yards, answering the bombs not with the sticks and stones that littered the ground, but with the defiant cry of "Afrika."

Police reinforcements began arriving. They came with six-wheeled Saracen armoured cars, which look like massive coffins, but which the Zulus call *isele* (frogs). Colonel Att Spengler, head of the South African police security branch for the Rand district, arrived.

In answer to an unseen leader, the crowd moved away from the entrance to the location and began a parade down the main street towards the municipal offices. The whistle music paced them and people were shouting "Afrika" and the Pan-Africanist slogan, "*Izwe lethu* (Our land)." It was not an angry mob but more like a mass celebration.

For some reason that remains unclear, the police turned to the South African Air Force for help; and at 11:40 A.M. Sabre jets arrived from Pretoria and dived on the crowd. They did not open fire, but depended on their screaming engines and low-flying passes to disperse the crowd. The aerial show of force made no impression at all. A few Africans brandished their fists at the Sabres, others threw their hats in the air. No one fled.

By noon the crowd had grown in size and, according to police, it was hostile. The police estimate was fifteen thousand Africans. The South African Department of External Affairs in Cape Town, nearly a thousand miles away, made it twenty thousand. The Pan-Africanists later adopted the twenty thousand figure as a testimonial to their organizing ability.

Independent evidence from the first two newspapermen on the scene—Humphrey Tyler, assistant editor of *Drum* magazine, and his chief photographer, Ian Berry—placed the crowd at between three thousand and five thousand. Tyler and Berry, who arrived at noon, also disagreed with police as to the crowd's mood. The newspapermen found the people grinning and cheerful. Berry's photographs tended to confirm their estimates both of the size and of the outlook of the demonstration.

Tyler and Berry arrived in the wake of Colonel Spengler and the Saracens. The police reinforcements headed for the police station deep inside the settlement. The hatches on the armoured cars were battened down and their crews looked out on Sharpeville through narrow slits in the armour plating.

"The Africans," said Tyler, "did not appear to be alarmed by the cars. Some looked interested. Some just grinned."

Tyler and Berry went behind the police station to park their car. "We could see a couple of Saracens, their tops poking starkly above the heads of the crowd, just over a hundred yards away from us. This was about seven minutes before the police opened fire.

"The crowd seemed to be loosely gathered around them and on the fringes people were walking in and out. The kids were playing. In all there seemed to be about three thousand people.

"They seemed amiable."

There were between one hundred and one hundred and fifty policemen in the station grounds. In front of the station was a five-foot wire fence, and behind that the crowd. Colonel Gideon Pienaar of the uniformed police was now in command.

Sergeant Grobler saw it this way: "We were only a handful against very many. I am quite certain they would have wiped us out. If they had flattened the fence nothing could have stopped them."

Grobler saw two Africans climb across the fence. Colonel Spengler sortied out of the police station, arrested one of the Africans, and took him inside the station. He went out again and captured a second African. A third Negro then entered the station grounds and Spengler went out again to get him.

"A struggle ensued," Grobler recalled. "Then the mob surged forward and almost flattened the fence around the police station. They started throwing stones at us."

Without orders, one policeman opened fire. He was one of a line of constables on the western side of the station grounds. They were armed with .38 revolvers, .303 rifles, and Sten guns.

Fifty-one other policemen began firing in bursts, pouring 476 bullets—according to the official report—into the crowd.

Sergeant Grobler said he heard no shots from the crowd, although the South African Department of External Affairs in Cape Town issued a statement: "The demonstrators shot first and the police were forced to fire in self-defence and to avoid even more tragic results."

Where they had parked, Tyler and Berry heard the shooting. In Tyler's words:

There were shrill cries of *"Izwe lethu"*—women's voices, I thought. The cries came from the police station and I could see a small section of the crowd swirl around the Saracens. Hands went up in the Africanist salute.

Then the shooting started. We heard the chatter of a machine-gun, then another, then another. The first rush was on us and then past.

There were hundreds of women, some of them laughing. They must have thought the police were firing blanks.

One woman was hit about ten yards from our car. Her companion, a young man, went back when she fell. He thought she had stumbled.

Then he turned her over and saw that her chest had been shot away. He looked at the blood on his hand and said: "My God, she's gone!"

Hundreds of kids were running too. One little boy had on an old black coat, which he held up behind his head, thinking, perhaps, that it might save him from the bullets. Some of the children, hardly as tall as the grass, were leaping like rabbits. Some of them were shot, too.

Still the shooting went on. One of the policemen stood on top of a Saracen, and it looked as though he was firing his Sten gun into the crowd. He was swinging it around in a wide arc from his hip as though he were panning a movie camera. Two other police officers were on the truck with him, and it looked as if they were firing pistols.

Most of the bodies were strewn in the road running through the field in which we were. One man who had been lying still, dazedly got to his feet, staggered a few yards then fell in a heap. A woman sat with her head cupped in her hands.

One by one the guns stopped. Nobody was moving in our field except Berry. The rest were wounded or dead. There was no longer a crowd and it was very quiet.

Before the shooting, I heard no warning to the crowd to disperse. There was no warning volley. When the shooting started it did not stop until there was no living thing on the huge compound in front of the police station.

The police have claimed that they were in desperate danger because the crowd was stoning them. Yet only three policemen were reported to have been hit by stones—and more than two hundred Africans were shot down.

The police also have said that the crowd was armed with "ferocious weapons" which littered the compound after they fled.

I saw no weapons, although I looked very carefully, and afterwards studied the photographs of the death scene. While I was there, I saw only shoes, hats and a few bicycles left among the bodies.

It seems to me that tough stuff was behind the killings at Sharpeville. The crowd gave me no reason to feel scared, though I moved among them without any distinguishing mark to protect me, quite obvious with my white skin.

I think the police were scared, though, and I think the crowd knew it.

That final shrill cry from the women before the shooting started certainly sounded much more like a jeer than a battle-cry. And the first Africans who fled past me after the shooting started were still laughing.

It was all over by 1:30 P.M. Within ten minutes four or five ambulances arrived. The dead were taken away in trucks. Stunned police constables gently helped the injured on to stretchers. In Vereeniging, shocked whites organized an emergency blood-transfusion service.

The first bulletin from Sharpeville landed on my desk at *The Toronto Star* about 9 A.M. (South African time is seven hours in advance of Eastern Standard.) It was a brief announcement by a police brigadier that about thirty and possibly more Africans had been shot down during a riot. Later reports described the use of diving Sabre jets to try and disperse the crowd. Gradually the death toll mounted until it reached sixty-six.

The early news-agency dispatches were fragmentary, and at the morning news conference it was decided I should telephone South Africa to obtain a more complete picture of the massacre. I placed a call to the news editor of the *Rand Daily Mail* in Johannesburg, but was told that it could not be completed until 8 A.M. the following day.

By the time of the afternoon news conference, the news agencies had filled in more details of the day's events, but two questions were left unanswered: Was it necessary for the police to shoot down more than two hundred Africans? Was this the beginning of a major revolt of Negroes against the system of white supremacy?

For nearly a dozen years it had become common to refer to the South African Government as stubborn men sitting on top of a volcano. There was no doubt anywhere outside South Africa that the volcano would one day erupt. Was the Sharpeville massacre the signal for an explosion that would shatter the cruel doctrine of Apartheid?

Before the day of Monday, March 21, was out, I was on board a plane carrying me the 10,000 miles from Toronto to Johannesburg. In the following four weeks before my return, I was to see the race problems of South Africa at first hand.

I was to be stoned by African gangsters and come as close to death as I had been since the Second World War. And I was to be jailed by the South African Nationalist Government for reporting the ugly details of the repulsive doctrine of Apartheid.

2. BACKGROUND

APARTHEID (pronounced apart-ate) is a Dutch or Afrikaans word meaning "apartness," "separateness," or, broadly, "segregation." Afrikaans is the language that the seventeenth-century Netherlanders developed after their arrival in South Africa. It differs from modern Dutch as the result of a different environment and the incorporation of Hottentot, Bantu, Malay, and Portuguese words.

Jan van Riebeeck, a Dutch ship's surgeon, landed at Table Bay on the Cape of Good Hope in April, 1652, and established a station where the fleet of the Dutch East India Company could obtain fresh provisions. Thirty-six years later they were joined by Huguenots driven out of France by Louis XIV.

The Africans living in the Cape area during van Riebeeck's day were Hottentots and Bushmen. Today's survivors of the Bushmen are still a Stone Age people living in the Kalahari desert. Few pure Hottentots remain; many were killed off in an eighteenth-century smallpox epidemic, others were absorbed by the early Dutch community, so small in numbers that intermarriage was encouraged.

With Malays, imported by the Dutch from the East Indies as slave labour, the Hottentots became the ancestors of the 1,360,000-strong Coloured (meaning mulatto or half-caste) community of today. The strain also derives from visiting white sailors, but the Coloured people rarely married the Bantu Negroes.

Bantu, in the language of Apartheid, is used to refer to all Negroes in South Africa, whatever their tribal background. Correctly used, Bantu refers to a number of peoples, including the Matabele, the Zulu, and the Swahili, who speak a similar language. Because of its incorporation in the legal terminology of Apartheid, Bantu has become in African ears only slightly less offensive than the derogatory Kaffir.

The early Dutch settlers did not encounter the Bantu until the first *trekboers* (itinerant farmers) left the Cape settlement and moved out to carve their own farms and ranches. The *trekboers* then ran into the warlike Xhosas and other tribes. After many frontier-type skirmishes between the Dutch and the Africans, a settlement was made in 1776 on the line of the Great Fish River, less than two hundred miles north-east of Cape Town. Raids and counter-raids across this dividing line led to the first of a series of Kaffir wars in 1779.

The British entered in 1795 when they seized the Cape from the Dutch in order to protect shipping routes to India and the East. Britain's right to the Cape was confirmed in the Treaty of Paris (1814) and British settlers began moving in. They spread out from Cape Town along the Indian Ocean coast in the direction of Natal.

South Africa became a struggle for domination among Briton, Boer, and African. Under pressure from the British, the Boers headed northward in the Great Trek that brought them into conflict with the Zulus. The Trek was a magnificent episode, outshining the wagon trains that made their way westward across North America.

The motives for the Great Trek were a mixture of seeking freedom from British rule, finding new lands to replace worn-

out farms, and re-establishing a way of life that included
slavery, recently outlawed under the law of Britain. The trek
not only emphasized the division between Boer and Briton,
but it also cut off the Boer from progress in the outside world.

The Trekkers established the South African Republic
(now the Transvaal) and the Orange Free State, and they
might have been able to live their fundamentalist lives in
isolation had it not been for the discovery of diamonds on the
Orange River and of gold on the Witwatersrand. From modest agricultural states, the Boer Republics turned into rich
prizes. The inevitable result was the Boer War.

The Boer War (1899-1902) united South Africa politically,
but at the price of lasting racial divisions. "More than any
other single event," says Dr. C. W. de Kiewiet, president of
the University of Rochester, New York, "the Boer War intensified, complicated and embittered the already ensnarled
relationships of Boer and Briton, Bantu and Indian, white
and non-white."

The fact that 26,000 Boer women and children died in
British detention camps during the Boer War was not allowed to be forgotten. The generosity of the postwar settlement and the 1909 Act of Union were overlooked. Although
the new Union of South Africa never has had an Englishman
as prime minister the spirit of reconciliation was not allowed
to flourish.

General Botha, the union's first prime minister, and Gen.
Smuts were regarded by unforgiving Afrikaner die-hards as
faithless traitors. Botha and Smuts wanted to turn their
backs on the past and build a South African nation with a
unified European community, that would have a distinctive
character neither Dutch nor English.

Smuts went a long way towards this goal, but a hard core

of Afrikaner irreconcilables slowly built a philosophy and a following for their own bigoted, aggressive nationalism. They chafed under the supremacy of the English language and worked energetically to establish Afrikaans on an equal level officially. (Until 1925, the Union's official languages were English and Dutch.)

Afrikaner nationalism grew in strength as British prestige diminished between the two world wars. Nationalist extremists formed links with Nazi Germany, and by 1939 were hoping for British defeat that would permit the establishment of an independent Afrikaner republic.

The nationalist philosophers looked back to the two Boer Republics that had established a society based on cheap land and cheap labour. The labour was provided by a subjugated native population that was segregated socially and denied political rights.

Reinforcing this view was the Afrikaner's version of Calvinism, which withholds the full grace of God from the native. This became the religious justification for Apartheid—the Afrikaner were a chosen people with a manifest destiny to rule South Africa. God had given the African his inferior position, and it would be wrong for the master race even to hold out hope to the black man of improvement in his status.

The Dutch Reformed churches—there are three of them—provided the scriptural argument for Apartheid. One of their ministers went to the length of ruling that while white and black shared a heritage of original sin, the black people inherited a greater propensity for sinning.

Afrikaner nationalism opened war on two fronts—against cultural and political domination from the British, and to maintain white supremacy, which they felt was threatened by the African. The nationalist solution was maximum separation of races, languages, and cultures.

One of the first goals was political power. The Afrikaners outnumbered the English-speaking South Africans by a ratio of six to four. The problem was to unite all Afrikaners under one party. A start was made in 1912 by General James Barry Munnik Hertzog, who formed the Nationalist party.

Hertzog believed Boer and Briton should develop along separate lines. He became Prime Minister in 1924, established Afrikaans on an equal basis with English, and introduced the Union flag. Hertzog joined Smuts in the 1933 coalition government, but the ardent Afrikaner nationalists did not follow him. They found a new leader in Dr. Daniel François Malan.

When Smuts brought South Africa into the Second World War on the side of Britain, Hertzog left the coalition and rejoined Malan. Hertzog actively hated Africans, and earned the title of father of Apartheid; but he died during the war and it was Malan who won the election of 1948 and carried out the policy of white supremacy.

The 1948 Malan government was the first all-Afrikaner administration in South African history. It gained office partly as the result of the system of representation favouring the underpopulated rural areas that were Nationalist strongholds, but mainly on the promise to solve the country's racial problems according to the traditional Boer policy of *baasskap* or white ascendancy.

Malan promised to separate the races in schools, residential areas, occupations, and in any other way necessary to assert white supremacy. He began by repealing the recently granted Parliamentary representation for the Union's 400,000 Indians. Immigration was curtailed, because few immigrants could be found who would accept, or be accepted by, the Afrikaner Nationalists. Most newcomers voted for Gen. Smuts's United Party.

Resistance to Apartheid was treason, said Johannes Gerhardus Strijdom, Malan's lieutenant who later succeeded him. The Minister of Education demonstrated his loyalty to this doctrine by cutting down grants for feeding African schoolchildren.

The real work of erecting the legal structure of Apartheid began in 1949. Entry into twenty-one cities and towns for the purpose of seeking work was forbidden to all Africans. The Mixed Marriages Act and the Immorality Amendment Act, 1950, forbade marriages between Europeans and non-Europeans as well as any sexual relationship between Europeans and non-whites. To buttress this legislation, it was necessary to institute the Population Registration Act classifying the entire population by racial groups.

Race classification was carried out by such scientific methods as running a comb through a subject's hair to determine whether he should fall into the Coloured or the Negro category. Informers were encouraged to accuse people of having impure blood in their veins.

Segregation on trains and buses and in public places was decreed by the Separate Amenities Act. It became a crime to support any campaign for the repeal or modification of any law.

The Minister of Labour was empowered to determine what occupations the members of any race might engage in. Under this authority skilled jobs were reserved for whites, so that the burden of unemployment would be reserved for the Africans. Men with black skins were banned from bricklaying, operating elevators, or driving anything larger than a three-ton truck.

The Group Areas Act divides the entire country into racial areas, and decrees that whites, Coloured, and Africans must live in separate areas. Inspectors are given the right to enter any dwelling without notice, by day or night, to see that the Act is carried out. According to the terms of this law, persons of one group are not permitted to own or occupy property in a controlled area of another group. An African lawyer may not have his offices near the courts where white lawyers have their chambers; the African is restricted to a township or location a dozen or more miles away from the halls of justice where he must appear.

In Johannesburg, where there is an Indian population of 30,000, largely of merchants, the Group Areas Act will banish them to the bare veld twenty miles from the city. In Durban over 100,000 non-whites are to be moved, partly so that Africans will be able to travel from their homes outside the city to their places of work without polluting any white residential area by passing through it.

The Group Areas Act is one of the corner-stones of Apartheid. Not only was it the creation of the Nationalist Government, but it was supported by the official opposition—the United Party, now led by Smuts' ineffectual successor, Sir de Villiers Graaff. The United Party believes in economic integration, but it countenances social and residential segregation.

The Suppression of Communism Act makes the Minister of Justice sole arbiter of whether a person is a Communist or not. If the minister "deems" a person a Communist, he may compel him to resign from all societies and organizations, forbid him to enter certain areas, and ban him from speaking publicly. A "Communist" is automatically barred from any position in a trade union or in the public service.

Cultural associations that do not observe the colour bar face the loss of government grants. The Industrial Conciliation Act forbids the formation of multi-racial unions and denies Africans trade-union representation. (There are African trade unions, but they are not recognized and cannot engage in collective bargaining.)

The Bantu Education Act, sponsored by the present Prime Minister Hendrik Frensch Verwoerd, is another essential part of the Apartheid structure. Giving complete control of African education to the Government, the act effectively limits African aspirations. There was no place, Dr. Verwoerd announced, for Africans in the European community "above the levels of certain forms of labour." African students were to be taught in Bantu languages and given only enough instruction in Afrikaans and English to permit them to carry out orders.

The removal of 48,000 Coloured voters in Cape Province from the common electoral roll was accomplished by packing the Appellate Court (increasing its membership from five to eleven) and packing the Senate (increasing the number of senators from forty-eight to eighty-nine and giving the Government seventy-seven of the seats).

After laying the foundations of Apartheid and erecting its legal structure, the Nationalists under Malan, Strijdom, and Verwoerd plastered the statute books with laws patching up gaps in the hideous edifice. When South Africans began criticizing Apartheid while they were outside the country, the Departure from the Union Regulation Act was passed to withhold passports from persons whom the Government considered might make harmful statements if they travelled outside the Union.

To avoid the calamity of a registered African nurse giving orders to a trained or untrained European, the Nursing Act ordered separate racial registers and placed the profession under an all-white council. There had been some embarrassment when some African nurses in postgraduate courses in Britain outscored Afrikaner girls. That would be corrected under the new Act, permitting the white nursing council to prescribe different courses for different races.

The Criminal Law Amendment Act provides penalties of $840 and/or three years and/or lashes for protest against the laws of Apartheid. Incitement to protest can be punished by a fine of $1,400 and/or five years and/or lashes.

The Public Safety Act enables the Government to proclaim emergency regulations under which the Minister of Justice, a magistrate, or a commissioned police officer can order the detention of anyone without warrant, charge, or trial. (It was under these regulations that I was to be detained in Durban prison as punishment for reporting the true state of affairs within South Africa.)

Some of the framework for Apartheid was long-standing. Nor was it entirely Afrikaner-inspired. The treatment of the Indians in Natal by the English-speaking South Africans has been as callous as the Afrikaner dealings with the Africans. The Natal Indians were originally imported to work on sugar plantations. In Natal, a white man may invite an Indian to his home but it is illegal to offer him a drink.

Some of the white-supremacy laws were already part of the South African way of life long before 1948. In 1921 a commission appointed under the Smuts government declared that towns were the preserves of the white people and that

the African "should only be allowed to enter urban areas
... when he is willing to enter and minister to the needs of
the white man, and should depart therefrom when he ceases
to minister."

The pass laws trace their development back to the days
of slavery. The racialist contribution to them has been the
harshness of their application. It is not uncommon for police
to haul people out of their beds in the middle of the night to
ask for passes. The excuse is "Just checking," but the practice is designed to remind the Negro of his inferior status.

Half the South African police force is estimated to be per-
manently engaged in enforcing pass laws. The most common
offence comes under Section Ten of the Urban Areas Act,
controlling the influx of Africans into towns and cities. This
section states that the only African with a right to live in an
urban area for more than seventy-two hours is one who has
lived continuously in the area since birth; who has worked
there continually for ten years for one employer, or has been
a lawful resident for fifteen years.

Any African can be banished from the urban areas by an
official. When banished Negroes went to court to appeal these
orders, the Government created the Natives (Prohibition of
Interdicts) Act, which forbids the courts to hear the appeal
until the victim has removed himself from the cities. Even
if the banishment order was served on the wrong person,
the subject must leave for some South African Siberia before
attempting legal proceedings.

Some laws and regulations are purely vindictive; others
are accompanied by homilies describing the plight of the
native population. The Native Laws Commission of 1948
frankly describes the urbanization process for the African:
"The majority of such locations are a menace to the health

of the inhabitants ... disgrace ... quite unfit for human habitation ... mere shanties, often nothing more than hovels ... dark and dirty ... encumbered with unclean and useless rubbish ... one could hardly imagine more suitable conditions for the spread of tuberculosis."

It would be a mistake to ignore the fact that the intellectual theoreticians of Apartheid realize the extent of the South African mess. There is a vast body of literature—commission reports, social studies, and statistical analyses—concerning the nation's economic, political, and social conditions. There are sincere men among the Afrikaner Nationalists who think that Apartheid provides for the future development of the African and believe they are acting as much in the black man's interest as in their own.

The apologists for Apartheid work from the false assumption that white and non-white peoples are culturally incompatible. Some of them say they are prepared to pay the price of total separation of the two races and do without the services of the African. Dr. Verwoerd himself employs no Negro help in his household. But it is doubtful whether any South African government could impose total Apartheid on the country. The white South African's standard of living is firmly based on a supply of cheap black labour.

Even granting Dr. Verwoerd a measure of sincerity for his unctuous claim that Apartheid has been imposed in the interest of the Africans as much as in the interest of the whites, it cannot be denied that the mass of his supporters are hate-filled racial bigots. Dr. Verwoerd mouths the fancy phrases; his supporters want only "to keep the Kaffir in his place," and most of them are ready to achieve that end with either whip or gun.

Not all Afrikaners follow the Nationalist line on Apartheid.

Black Star

Sharpeville, March 21, 1960. Crowds of Africans start to flee when the police open fire. Many are laughing, thinking that the police are firing blanks. But by nightfall . . .

Black Star

Wide World

. . . sixty-seven lie dead and many more nurse bullet-wounded bodies.

United Press International

March 28 was proclaimed a Day of National Mourning by the African National Congress to honor the victims of the Sharpeville massacre. These pictures were taken in Orlando, a "model township" outside Johannesburg.

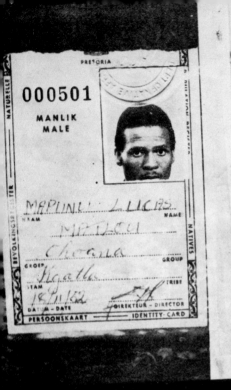

000501

MANLIK
MALE

NATURELLE · NATIVE

BYSOLANDSE · RESIDENTIAL

PRETORIA

NAAM / NAME: MSPUNU LUCAS

MPTLCH

GROEP / GROUP: Choana

STAM / TRIBE: Ngathe

DATUM / DATE: 18 11 52

DIREKTEUR · DIRECTOR

PERSOONSKAART — IDENTITY · CARD

Wide World

This is a *dompass* ("accursed pass") all Africans must carry, one of the factors contributing to the Sharpeville protest that brought on the massacre.

On the Day of Mourning an African woman at Johannesburg holds up her charred pass book.

Wide World

The "Tausa dance" African prisoners must perform nude to show that nothing is hidden on their persons. When *Drum* published this picture, which they obtained with some difficulty, the Government retaliated by passing a law forbidding anyone to photograph or describe jail life in South Africa.

An armoured car guarding the House of Parliament in Cape Town as a crowd of Africans marched to protest the arrest of their leaders.

Philip Kgosana leading the march.

K. Halim, Drum

The mile-long column.

Mr. Kgosana urged the crowd to disperse quietly, having made their protest.

K. Halim, Drum

South African troops threw tight cordons around Langa and Nyanga, townships near Cape Town.

A policeman with a long club chases a Negro in Langa.

While the ratio of Afrikaner to English is roughly sixty to forty, at the 1958 election the best the Nationalists could do was obtain a fifty-fifty division of the votes with the United Party. However, half the votes gave the Nationalists 103 seats to the United Party's fifty-three.

A few other background facts:

Estimated population of South Africa:

White	3,011,000
African	9,606,000
Asiatic	441,000
Coloured	1,360,000
Total	14,418,000

Estimated number of Africans living in urban areas: 2,500,000

Land distribution:

700,000 whites own and occupy 250,000,000 acres

6,000,000 Africans occupy 35,000,000 acres

3. EYEWITNESS TO APARTHEID

I FIRST TASTED the bitter fruits of Apartheid on Monday, March 28, 1960, the Day of National Mourning proclaimed by the African National Congress to honour the victims of the Sharpeville massacre.

I was lucky to escape alive.

The day previous, Sunday, I had spent at one of Johannesburg's gold mines. On a Sunday morning the right thing for a European visitor to the City of Gold to do is to visit a mine and watch the display of tribal dancing. It is an exciting spectacle, put on by the African miners who hew the gold that makes Jo'burg the richest metropolis in the Southern hemisphere.

The mine where I was a guest was the Durban Roodeport Deep Limited. The dances were staged on the floor of a circular enclosure accommodating several thousand spectators on concrete bleachers. On the sunny side, packed close together, were Africans on their day off from the mine. In the shade sat the comfortable white visitors, almost every one of them armed with a camera.

Before the dancers appeared the arena vibrated with rhythm—the throb of drums, sometimes mellow marimbas, and then the shrilling of flutes and tin whistles. The beat was simple but commanding, if occasionally monotonous.

Proudest of the groups were the Xhosas, whose ancestors

had fought the *trekboers* along the Great Fish River. Their well-muscled brown bodies rippled with movement as they went through an initiation dance. Traditionally costumed, they wore decorative plumes and tassels with brief kilts. Belts of small bells were strapped across their swelling chests and rattles were attached to their legs. The entire team of about forty dancers weaved backwards and forwards at the command of their leader's whistle, to reach a climax with a violent shimmying of the chest muscles that set the bells tinkling, while bare feet stamped the ground making the rattles quiver.

There are fifty-five tribes represented among the miners, and, as I watched, nearly a score of them had their turn in the arena. As a pageant it was the equal of the Welsh national eisteddfod or any of the magnificent Russian folk-dancing ensembles.

Suddenly in the midst of this enthralling entertainment I suffered an emotional shock. I looked at the sign in front of me: THROWING MONEY, CIGARETS, ETCETERA IS PROHIBITED. I looked around at the prosperous white spectators with their expensive cameras. We were not in an open-air theatre watching an exhibition of folk culture. We were at a zoo.

This was a zoo where the exhibits were human beings. DON'T FEED THE ANIMALS, the sign warned the visitors not to give them money or cigarets. The program went further: "Visitors must be suitably dressed. Topless sunsuits and abbreviated shorts are not considered suitable dress." White girls in brief costumes might excite primitive lusts, and the problem of sexual outlets for 300,000 mine workers cooped up in compounds for nine to eighteen months is serious.

Rome had its gladiators; Johannesburg has its displays of native dancing. Not only is the atmosphere zoo-like, but this

Sunday-morning exhibition is the epitome, the distilled essence, of Apartheid. This is how the extreme Nationalists would like to see the entire country function.

First, look at the white spectators. The tribal dancers encourage them in the delusion that the African is and always will be a savage. There is absolute lack of communication between audience and performers. This is a zoo, not a concert stage where artists and spectators are drawn together by music and dancing. In daily South African life there is this same gulf between white and black.

Now consider the dancers. They are miners brought to Johannesburg from all over the Union and from surrounding countries. The biggest airlift in the world is built on the transport of recruits from distant rural areas to the gold mines. About 70 per cent of them come from Basutoland, Portuguese colonies, Nyasaland, and other countries neighbouring South Africa.

These young Africans are hired on contracts committing them to work for anything between nine and eighteen months. About 250,000 of them work underground in temperatures that vary from bitter cold to intense heat of one hundred degrees and more. The mines go down to depths of eight thousand feet and more, some of them directly beneath the city of Johannesburg.

The miners are well fed and, despite the serious threat of tuberculosis and silicosis, some actually leave the mines in better physical condition than when they arrived. They are housed in compounds similar to army barracks, and these may be more adequate than the housing where they have been brought up; but the atmosphere is prison-like. The men are not confined to the compounds; they can obtain passes once a week to go into the city; but to keep them out of trouble they are given little money to spend.

Pay averages five cents an hour. According to the official Bulletin of Statistics, 482,145 African miners all over the Union earned in 1958 an average wage of $15.62 per month. No figures were given for the value of food, accommodation, footwear, and medical services provided. South Africans boast these are the highest wages paid Negro labour on the entire continent. They also can't refrain from boasting that some mines make a profit as high as $2,800,000 a month.

Cheap labour for mines, factories, and farms is the purpose of Apartheid. It is not practical to keep all the African workers for shops, factories, and homes cooped up in compounds. The next best thing is to segregate the Africans in suburbs, called locations or townships. Originally, the Africans who worked in the cities lived in shanty-town slums. Their homes were nailed together from rusty tin and wood salvaged from packing crates. Too many of these still exist; but the good exponents of Apartheid had a better idea. They set up locations ten to fifteen miles outside the cities and they spent millions of dollars building housing for Africans on these locations.

Orlando is one of the model townships outside Johannesburg. It was built at the cost of about $10,000,000 and it accommodates about 80,000 Africans. "All they want to do," a complacent police officer explained to us, "is drink, fight and have women. You must remember they are only savages."

In fact, Orlando is a cross-section of urban Africans—a mass of unskilled lower-class workers plus a sprinkling of middle-class lawyers, doctors, professional people, and merchants. The first two-story residence belonged to a wealthy witch doctor, but most of the homes were two-, three-, or four-room cottages. One long, low building, called the Shelters, consisted of a row of little rooms with one tap at the end of the row.

The location sprawls over rolling country stretching ten miles in either direction. It is covered with a network of roads, from paved main streets to winding dirt lanes. There is little electricity and even fewer telephones—they might serve politically minded Africans as a means of maintaining communication.

My first trip to Orlando was at noon on the Day of National Mourning. The police estimate of the number of Johannesburg's Africans who stayed home from work that day was 80 per cent. With Harold Sacks, the crime reporter for the Rand *Daily Mail,* and photographer Warwick Robinson I drove out to Orlando to sense the temper of the African strikers.

We passed the Baragwanath hospital, one of the biggest in Africa and restricted to African patients. It was in a state of siege, with uniformed and plain-clothes police guarding about 180 wounded victims from the Sharpeville massacre.

The hospital was on a main road south of Johannesburg, and just past it was the turning into Orlando. Near the entrance had once been scrawled an ominous greeting: ABANDON HOPE ALL YE WHO ENTER HERE. We were barely inside the location when we encountered a gang of teen-age Africans weaving their way down the road.

This was my introduciton to the *tsotsis,* the African juvenile delinquents spawned by Apartheid. Some have never known schooling, most of them have never found jobs. Work is difficult enough for an African to find, and the *tsotsi* preys on his fellow African, robbing or blackmailing him of his wages.

The boys who forced our car to a halt had been drinking, and had been smoking *dagga*, the local equivalent of marijuana or hashish. The drug had removed all inhibitions, and they hurled abuse and spittle at us, threatening to overturn the car.

We were driving a Canadian Ford of the same model used by the South African police, a mistake that was to get us into more serious trouble after dark. Robinson managed to edge the car through the gang and we headed for the police station.

Orlando was in turmoil. Gangs were ripping out the Rediffusion network of piped radio—it had become a symbol of white oppression. At street corners small groups gathered around burning pass books. Some of these had been seized from fellow Africans but many were burned in response to the example set the day previous by Chief Albert Luthuli of the African National Congress.

The day built up to a climax at 5 p.m., when the commuter trains began arriving from Johannesburg. Most of the cars were empty, but huddled in some were the few who, because of need or because they feared losing their jobs more than they feared the disapproval of their neighbours, had defied the strike call. The more militant Africans and the *tsotsis* were waiting for them on their return.

Stones clattered against the sides of the trains, and when the attacks started at Mzimhlophe station I drove to the scene with Robinson, Sacks, and a squad of South African police. The station straddled the tracks, with exits leading to settlements on either side of the line. Railway police armed with rifles were spaced out along the tracks. They were the targets for an occasional volley of stones from young Africans above them on the embankment.

The police—about twenty black constables armed with batons, under a white sergeant with a Sten gun—lined up across the road leading to the station. In front of them was a small band of about fifty young Africans. They were singing in their own language. The words began, I was told, "Africa must come back to us."

Unable to understand the words, I could only sense the song's rhythmic beat. The Africans danced as they sang. Their shuffling steps took them to within a few feet of the police ranks, then they would retreat. They defied and taunted the impassive constables in this fashion, then turned and danced their way down the road to the other side of the tracks. The song died away in the distance, only to come back as the crowd of demonstrators, now swollen to a couple of hundred, reappeared.

There were women with them now, keening a high-pitched war cry—"Lee-lee-lee-lee-lee." Under the hypnosis of rhythm they had danced and chanted away their fear of the police.

My mind went back to the tribal dancing at the mine compound the day before and its zoo-like atmosphere. But this was no Sunday-morning diversion. The animals were out of their cages. Only these were not animals; they were human beings, with hopes and aspirations as well as resentments and grievances.

Domineering Saracen armoured cars wheeled into the scene. The Africans replied with showers of stones, and I crouched in the lee of the cars as bits of rock rattled harmlessly against the armour and kicked up spurts of dust on the road around me.

Captain J. DeWet Steyn, commander of the Orlando police station, took charge of the situation and at the right moment dispersed the Africans with a baton charge. Steyn was an efficient policeman whom I had watched during most of the day. He never lavished the force at his disposal, and even the charge with batons flailing in the twilight gloom was carried out with a minimum of blows.

Steyn wisely withdrew the Saracens; they were two-edged weapons, as likely to provoke violence as to subdue it. As the situation stabilized he withdrew his men, leaving a small guard at the station itself. With darkness upon us, Robinson, Sacks, and I decided it was time to get out of the location and return to the city.

We headed back along the route we had taken to Mzimhlophe. There were small knots of Africans at every intersection. Approaching a main road junction, we interrupted a gang rolling boulders out to form a road-block. Robinson weaved the car through the unfinished barricade, and there was a heavy thud as a rock came singing out of the darkness and hit the car trunk.

Three minutes later another ambush forced us to change direction, and we left the only road out in favour of a rutted lane. We were travelling thirty to forty miles an hour but unsure of our directions.

From the side of the road a *tsotsi* stepped boldly into the car lights. In a split second we saw the softball-sized stone leave his hand, arcing its way into the windshield. It was like a slow-motion movie. The glass disintegrated into a gaping hole surrounded by the crazy pattern of shattered splinters. Fragments showered the inside of the car.

Robinson kept the wheel under control, holding the car to the road. Others were not so fortunate. One African driver stopped his car when his windshield was shattered. Gangsters hauled him out and beat him to death in a senseless orgy of violence.

We speeded away from the attack and soon found ourselves in a quiet sector of the location. Warning us that if anything should happen to him, we should drive off, Sacks got out of the car and gingerly approached an African home.

In a few minutes Sacks returned with an elderly man, who shook his head at the sight of the shattered windshield. He was as shocked as we at the *tsotsi* violence, and offered to accompany us until he could set us on the right road. It was a courageous offer for he would have to walk back to his home on a night when it was not safe for any man, white or black, to be on foot in Orlando.

After a mile he pointed to a street light in the distance and told us to take the second turn to the left. We thanked him for his kindness and watched him walk off into the darkness. An African-driven car passed us as we started off again. As he approached the intersection where we were to turn off, there was another crash of glass and metal. He had driven into ambush.

Robinson backed away furiously until we reached a track that led us away. By now we were utterly lost, with all sense of direction gone and not a landmark to be seen. The lights picked up an African father and his child. We risked stopping to ask directions. He was dumb to our request, unwilling rather than unable to assist us.

Another intersection and we turned left from instinct and encountered three matronly women, laundry on their heads, marching along in single file. They cheerfully told us how to find the police station, less than half a mile away.

The station was almost deserted, with every constable out on patrol. On one side of the location municipal buildings were burning, in another a church had been set alight. A railway station had been drenched with gasoline, but railway police arrived before it was set alight. The police radio blared out in harsh Afrikaans. One African constable had been knifed to death and two seriously injured. The lone sergeant in the station was methodically loading clips of ammunition for the Sten guns.

Gradually the patrols, in cars, trucks, and armoured cars, reported back to the station. A captain told me they had fired only once with the Stens and the shots over the crowd's heads were enough to disperse them. At 10 P.M. a small police car escorted us off the location. Everything was peaceful and not an African to be seen.

For some reason the horror of what I had been through did not strike me until the following morning in the safety of my hotel room, when I was writing my report on the Day of Mourning. I had no anger for the Orlando *tsotsis* who stoned me. Had I been an African I would have had a rock in my hand that night and I would have found me a police car as a target.

The horror was not in the personal danger but in the glimpse of unrestrained violence, as irresponsible gangsters took over the carefully planned non-violent demonstration called by responsible African political leaders.

The gangsters were masters of mayhem. They knew to the fraction of an inch where to knife a man in the spine so that he did not die but was condemned to the living death of a paraplegic. How long would it be before they learned the arts of guerrilla warfare—the use of the Molotov cocktail, made from gasoline, a bottle, and a piece of rag, that could reduce an armoured car to a charred coffin?

Would the African political leaders, dedicated to non-aggressive tactics, be able to hold these violent men in check? The South African Government knew the answer. Two days later they arrested every Negro leader on whom they could lay their hands, thereby offering the irresponsible elements their chance.

Fortunately, a few hours before he was jailed I was able to meet the most distinguished of the African leaders, Chief Albert John Luthuli, president of the African National Congress. The very next day, after being stoned by one group of Africans, I was to meet Chief Luthuli and find him the most intelligent of any South African, of any colour, whom I encountered.

4. ZULU CHIEF

WHEN I MET the Anglican Bishop of Johannesburg, the Right Reverend Ambrose Reeves, I told him that I had a teen-age daughter in Canada whose ambition was to come to South Africa and fight against Apartheid. "What," I asked the Bishop, "should I tell her about South Africa?"

Bishop Reeves is a warm, generous, and troubled man, a valiant fighter against racialism. He thought a moment and said: "Tell her about Chief Luthuli. My children idolize him."

Albert John Luthuli is a Zulu; the tribe's name means "People of Heaven," and nowhere have I met anyone who better fits that description. Chief Luthuli's strength and weakness is the Christian nobility of his character. He is president of the African National Congress, respected not only by his own people but also by many white South Africans, who see in him one of the few remaining ways to bridge the gap between the two communities.

The Nationalist Government has done everything in its power to destroy that possibility. They have jailed the chief on a treason charge, exiled him to a reservation farm, re-imprisoned him under the Emergency Regulations, and finally outlawed the A.N.C.

Chief Luthuli's nature showed itself in his statement fol-

lowing the Sharpeville massacre. After expressing his con-
dolences to the victims and their families, he said:

> I reiterate that the policy of the A.N.C. is one of non-
> violence and we have always done everything in our
> power to ensure its acceptance by the public, both
> Black and White.
>
> We urge upon the people to respect this policy.
>
> We would ask the authorities, however, not to resort
> to unnecessary violence in the performance of what they
> regard as their duty.
>
> No matter what differences in point of view exist be-
> tween the A.N.C. and the government, our role has al-
> ways been, and continues to be, one of the restraint of
> violence in the explosive situations which racial tensions
> have tended to create in our common fatherland.

Chief Luthuli was born sixty-one years ago in Rhodesia,
but he belongs to a clan of the Zulus called the Amalala, who
once owned a large section of present-day Durban, but now
dwell on the ten-thousand-acre Umvoti mission reserve about
forty miles north of the city. His father was an African
Christian missionary who was sent from Natal to Rhodesia
by the Congregationalist church in the United States.

Young Albert Luthuli was educated at Adams College,
then staffed by U.S. missionaries who dispensed first-class
training now denied Africans under the Bantu Education
Act. He later taught at Adams himself in the fields of music,
teacher training, geography, history, and the language of his
people.

In 1936 Luthuli was elected chief by his community and
with the approval of the Government. According to tradition,
the chief was elected for life, but with the understanding
that if he failed to respect the wishes of the people, another
election could be held for the purpose of removing him.

Strictly speaking, he is now Ex-Chief Luthuli. The South African Government ousted him from office in 1952 as punishment for his part in that year's defiance campaign organized by the African National Congress. As Congress president, he was summoned to the capital in Pretoria and lectured by his white masters. The authorities gave him two weeks in which to resign from the Congress movement, on pain of removal from the government-paid appointment as chief.

Chief Luthuli quietly explained the principles of a Zulu chief. His first duty is to his people, and his second as a government official. He was immediately dismissed; but his people were so proud of him that they refused to elect anyone in his place.

With the chieftainship, Luthuli lost his source of income and was forced to go on the land. He now calls himself a "peasant farmer" and regrets, for his wife's sake, that Congress work and jail do not allow time either for efficient farming or for uninterrupted home life.

His farm is near Groutville, a town named after an American missionary. A condition of his 1952 banishment made it an offence for him to attend public gatherings including church services; but this did not stop him preaching in the local church.

The original banishment was lifted, and in 1959 it was possible for Chief Luthuli to travel to the principal cities of the Union. He began addressing meetings that attracted large audiences of all races. Africans would arrive early and fill the halls where he was to appear. It was typical of African courtesy that these early birds would surrender their seats to white people who arrived closer to the scheduled opening time. The chief's success with these mixed audiences angered the Government, and a new banishment order restricted him to the reservation.

It is an offence for a white man to visit the chief's twenty-five-acre farm. When his daughter was married, a missionary friend who had been invited by the chief had to obtain a special permit to attend. This document stipulated that the missionary could attend the wedding, but specifically barred him from joining in any of the social activities. The missionary was also ordered to take with him his own supply of food.

Durban once had an international house where people of different colours could meet. This place was closed down by the Government. It was an offence for a white person to meet the chief, or any other person of colour, in any hotel or restaurant. Fortunately for me, the Government had lifted the ban on Chief Luthuli temporarily, so that he could appear as a witness at the fantastic treason trial that was limping through its third year in a deconsecrated synagogue in Pretoria.

It was before dawn in the early hours of December 5, 1956, that this weird legal process began. By breakfast time that morning the Special Branch of the South African police had arrested 140 men and women, white, Negro, Indian and mulatto, and charged them with high treason against the State. Within the following three weeks the total of arrests reached 156, including Chief Luthuli.

There was no court big enough to hold all the accused, and the preliminary examination was held in a Johannesburg armoury. The prisoners were placed inside a wire enclosure nicknamed the cage; they couldn't hear what the magistrate was saying, and the magistrate could not see what was going on at the rear of the enclosure where it faced the spectators.

Some of the more light-hearted of the accused used this opportunity to pass out notes to the press saying, "Please do not feed the animals."

The preliminary examination lasted a little more than one year. At the end of it 65, including Chief Luthuli, were discharged. This left 91, and their trial proper started August 1, 1958, in the old Pretoria Synagogue with its onion-shaped steeples.

On the first day defence counsel I. A. Maisels, Q.C., successfully challenged the presence of one of the three red-robed justices. Mr. Justice Ludorf disqualified himself on the grounds that he had acted in a previous case involving one of the prisoners but had forgotten all about it. It took another week to find a replacement for the judge.

Maisels then attacked the wording of the indictment, and after two and a half months of legal argument, the prosecution withdrew it for rewording. The accused were split into smaller groups and another start made on January 1959. By the end of the year, it was estimated that 4,500,000 words had gone into the record.

The most ludicrous testimony was provided by the Government's expert on Communism, a Professor Murray, whose definition turned out to be a catch-all defining as Red anyone who approved of even the most modest reform advocated by the Communist party.

Defence counsel read to Professor Murray an extract from a book and asked him whether he considered the author a Communist. The professor had no hesitation in dubbing the writer Communistically inclined. Counsel then informed him that the author of the passage in question was none other than Professor Murray himself.

Waiting for the bus in Johannesburg that would take me

to the trial in Pretoria about thirty miles away, I struck up a conversation with an Afrikaner who turned out to be on the staff of the university of Pretoria. I made no secret of being an "overseas journalist," although Afrikaners are conditioned by their papers to regard any newspaperman from abroad as a perverted liar. The university man undertook to brief me on the racial situation. The basic thing to remember, he said, was that all Africans were savages and that however much education they absorbed, they remained uncivilized. Once they heard the war drums they would tear off their clothes and reveal their primitive natures. Even Chief Luthuli could not escape the call of blood.

My instructor was himself a cultured and kindly man. When we reached Pretoria he took me to the tourist bureau to find out where the treason trial was going on and insisted on escorting me to the doors, although it was half a dozen blocks out of his way. He invited me to his home that evening, a gesture that I had to refuse because I was returning to Johannesburg.

The first thing that struck me as I entered the temple was the bench with its row of three justices in scarlet robes. They were listening gravely, like three images in a tableau. The prosecutor stood a full twenty feet away from them, at the bottom of a U-shaped table that opened towards the bench. At the prosecutor's right and a dozen feet away, a witness stood in what looked like a small pulpit. He was Chief Luthuli.

The chief radiated a natural dignity. Their robes and trappings gave the justices a commanding aspect, but one could imagine them leaving court in ordinary clothes—three ordinary and insignificant men. The black-gowned prosecutor was trying to bait Chief Luthuli into admitting that he advocated force. The chief deftly handled his questions with the bored professionalism of a veteran theologian refuting an earnest young agnostic. (Later, Luthuli told me he regretted his own lack of patience, but at the end of a long day in court, the badgering of the prosecution exhausted his forbearance.)

Outside the court Chief Luthuli strode to a waiting car with a stately walk. He was a tall man, with the robust chest and vocal equipment of the Zulus, who in the rolling country-side can converse with one another over half a mile of distance. There were touches of grey in his hair and moustache, but his face broke easily into a grin that was almost boyish.

He wore a black rosette on his lapel that I mistook as a mourning symbol for Sharpeville's dead. Grinning, the chief explained that it was nothing of the sort. It was a mourning band, he said, but he had been wearing it to mark the Union of South Africa's fiftieth anniversary—fifty years of oppression.

The instinct for humour showed itself again when we discussed the country's history. I had heard Prime Minister Verwoerd declare that if the white man had not come to South Africa, the Negroes would have killed themselves off in tribal wars.

"Perhaps you will tell Doctor Verwoerd for me," said Luthuli, "that he should study the history of our country again. My people did not write the histories. They were written by his people, and they show that it was the white man who set tribe against tribe. Why, the Afrikaners in the early days assisted one rebellious prince in a revolt that made him King of the Zulus."

Dr. Verwoerd's version of South African history is that the country was empty when the whites moved north from the Cape while the Bantu descended from Central Africa.

The suggestion is that the white man got to this virgin territory before the black.

"Our people," said the chief, "first met the Boers along the Great Fish River where the first Kaffir War was fought, less than two hundred miles from Cape Town." Again the grin broke out. "You can also tell Dr. Verwoerd that if he would like to partition the country along this line where we first met, I should be happy to accept." (Such a division, of course, would leave the Africans in possession of the immensely rich gold and diamond fields as well as a major part of the country.)

It was not surprising to hear that Dr. Verwoerd has never met with the man who is president of the African National Congress (membership between 50,000 and 100,000). The Nationalist leaders have vowed never to consult with the African leaders. However, it was hard to believe that this wise and able man had never met any of the opposition United Party leaders. "Until the Progressive party was formed last year," he said, "I had never had the privilege of meeting any member of Parliament."

Of the average white South African, Chief Luthuli said, "They really don't know how we live. Neither Afrikaners nor English have any contact with us except on the basis of master and servant. And the man who is a servant knows how far he can go while talking to his master. We have a saying, 'A suggestion from your master is as good as law.'

"Why, even one of the Nationalist papers the other day said, 'We must find out what these people want.'

"I like to think well of White South Africa. I hope that when we exert enough pressure through the A.N.C. and our campaign of non-violence and passive resistance, the whites will discuss our problems with us. I like to think that the continent of Africa, which is in the process of developing, will lead the way in showing how people of different races can live together. That could be our contribution to history."

Not a trace of bitterness or rancor escaped him. It almost made me wonder whether he appreciated the Nationalists' capacity for brutality and vindictiveness. I had been recently in Algeria, where the French and the Algerian Nationalists have been fighting a bitter war for more than five years.

"I can't see that happening here," said Luthuli. "We don't like to appear to be angels, but it just isn't a practical proposition."

Two days previously, Chief Luthuli had burned his pass book publicly. It was a typical gesture, neatly timed as a response to the national chief of police's announcement that enforcement of pass laws was to be suspended temporarily. But the chief knew that his defiant example would only be successful if enough of his people did the same thing. If only 500,000 of the country's 9,600,000 Africans burned their passes, he realized that the government could and might easily arrest those half million people.

We were sitting on the verandah of the chief's host in Pretoria, John Brink, a white man who was chairman of the local branch of the Liberal party. Brink was to pay for his hospitality and for his political views by being cast into jail the next day under the Emergency Regulations.

Breaking into our conversation about passes, Brink pointed to the street running past his garden, and told of witnessing an accident in which an African on a bicycle was knocked down. Brink telephoned both for an ambulance and the police. A constable was the first to arrive at the scene. "The first thing he did," Brink recalled, "was to prod the injured man and ask him for his pass."

The chief nodded. "You can't know what it is to live under the pass system," he said, "unless you have been forced to carry one."

Ending the pass system is one of the immediate goals of the Congress. Its main aims are:

1. To protect and advance the interests of the African people in all matters affecting them.

2. To attain the freedom of the African people from all discriminatory laws whatsoever.

3. To strive and work for the unity and co-operation of the African peoples in every possible way.

4. A Bill of Rights beginning, "We, the African people in the Union of South Africa, urgently demand the granting of full citizenship rights, such as are enjoyed by all Europeans in South Africa."

At its inception in 1912, Chief Luthuli explained, the Congress set out to organize the African people into a united group that would replace the tribal categories into which they were split. The authorities, of course, were anxious to keep them divided. Originally the Congress restricted itself to presenting the Government with its aspirations and grievances, but in the forties it began to make political demands.

"We want a stake in the government of our country," the chief said. "We want the vote on a universal franchise—one man, one vote—civil rights, and all democracy has to give. We are at war with discrimination and racialism."

Luthuli is a gradualist. Like many of his generation, he speaks of achieving these goals "in our lifetime." If the Government would negotiate with the Congress, Luthuli would compromise—possibly accepting as a first step a vote for Africans with property or educational qualifications. This is what he means by negotiation; and the tragedy of South

Africa is the refusal of the Nationalists to recognize grievances, let alone discuss them with moderate African leaders.

As is to be expected, a younger generation of Africans has
produced leaders who have broken away from Luthuli's
leadership. These are the Pan-Africanists, who make similar
demands to those of the A.N.C., but with an ultimatum attached—human and political rights for all by 1963.

The Pan-Africanist Congress with its more militant policies
is taking away members from the A.N.C. Chief Luthuli
showed the same compassionate attitude towards the rival
group as he does towards the racialists. "I hesitate to be
categorical about our differences with the Pan-Africanists,"
he said. "They haven't defined their stand precisely. However, they are rallying around a type of African nationalism
that led them to expel a member for addressing a meeting
of the white Liberal party. This is a narrow view. We feel
it should be a South Africa of all races."

Brink and Luthuli drove me to the bus stop. In the flurry
of parting I asked the chief if he had anything he would like
to say to North Americans. He thought a moment and then
said, "I think the countries sympathetic to our cause should
get the facts. I don't want emotional sympathy. Then they
should use their influence with their governments so that
those governments, at the United Nations and other world
forums, will condemn the racial policies of our country."

I had to run for the bus. Chief Luthuli called after me,
"That's my last interview for a long time." There was a
cheerful grin and I thought he was joking.

Exactly nine hours later, at 2 A.M., this gentle yet imposing man was routed out of bed by the South African police
and carted off to Pretoria's Central Prison, to be held at the
pleasure of the Minister of Justice.

An uncouth prison warder slapped him about the head as he stood patiently in a line-up.

Central Prison, where Chief Luthuli was imprisoned on March 30, 1960, is a grim ordeal for a man of sixty-one suffering from high blood pressure. This is a description of the place from a letter smuggled out from one of his fellow-prisoners:

> We are kept five in a cell—our cells measure seven by ten feet. We sleep on mats with two blankets each. We have two buckets—one with water for drinking, washing, etc., and the other to be used as a latrine. We have to live day and night in the stench. We are allowed to empty them each morning. All the detainees here are never brought together. We just manage sometimes to see our immediate cell neighbours for a few minutes. We are kept locked up in our cells the whole day excepting for fifteen minutes every day when we are allowed to exercise our bodies.
>
> We get up at 5:30 A.M.—breakfast at 6:30 (porridge every day)—lunch at 11 A.M. (maize without salt) and supper at 2 P.M. (beans and porridge). Once or twice a week we are given about two ounces of meat each. The Sunday routine was much the same excepting that we had supper by about twelve noon. Needless to say, the blankets and mats are vermin infested.

This is how that bastion of Western civilization, South Africa, treats a truly dedicated Christian.

Four weeks after his incarceration as a menace to public safety, Chief Luthuli was fetched before the interminable treason trial. He took his place in the witness pulpit.

One of the accused, Duma Nokwe, addressed the court. He explained that his fellow prisoners were unanimous in their feeling that they could not expect a fair trial. Under the Emergency Regulations witnesses feared to testify in case they might incriminate themselves. Under these circumstances, it had been decided it would be a waste of money (the trial has already cost more than $500,000) to continue paying lawyers for the defence.

Mr. Nokwe is himself a lawyer, and he called the judges' attention to the South African law that permits accused to have the proceedings translated into their mother tongue. Some of the prisoners were Xhosa and Sesuto, and they wished to assert their right to having the hearings translated into their languages.

An interpreter was found, a former chief examiner of interpreters. (In the schizophrenic condition of South Africa there is either painstaking respect for the letter of the law or utter contempt for it.) Chief Luthuli took up the pattern of his testimony where he had left off a month previously.

Speaking fluent English, the chief launched into the historical background of the A.N.C. and an exposition of its philosophy of non-violence. The interpreter stumbled along behind him, trying to put the measured English phrases into Xhosa. When he floundered to a halt, Chief Luthuli would courteously provide the missing word. Sometimes he would suggest a correction of the interpretation.

By that time I also had had a taste of a South African jail, and had been expelled for trying to report the facts that Chief Luthuli suggested people in other countries should know. But my dearest wish would have been to be present in that Pretoria synagogue to salute that courageous and kindly representative of the "People of Heaven," Chief Albert John Luthuli.

5. LETTER TO A TEEN-AGE DAUGHTER

REBECCA WEST described Chief Luthuli as "whole African and whole Christian," a man with "the apostolic face." I was haunted by my memory of him, and of his Christianity that was summed up in the protest he made at his dismissal from chieftainship.

"Who will deny," he asked, "that thirty years of my life have been spent knocking in vain, patiently, moderately, at a closed and barred door? What have been the fruits of moderation?"

This was not his farewell to the creed of peaceful protest, but a reaffirmation of his dedication to non-violent methods.

In addition to following Bishop Reeves' advice to tell my daughter about Chief Luthuli, I also wrote her this letter:

Dear Susan:

You once said that one of your ambitions when you were older was to come to South Africa and fight Apartheid. Now that I have been in this very beautiful but unhappy country, I can give you a better idea of what Apartheid really means.

You remember that our family doctor in London, England, was David Pitt, who came from Trinidad and who is as black as a man can be. In South Africa David would not be allowed to have white patients. He would be allowed to work in a hospital for Africans along with white doctors;

he could operate on someone with the help of a white doctor, but he could not use the same bathroom outside the operating theatre as his white colleague. And white doctors get into trouble if they make a practice of entertaining their black colleagues.

You can't get away from Apartheid even when you are looking for sport or entertainment. Football, cricket, and tennis teams are always of one race. There is even a special law forbidding mixed bowling. When you go swimming, the beaches are segregated so that the white people are restricted to one and Africans to another; and there is a third area for "Coloureds," who are the descendants of mixed marriages. The segregation lines stretch three miles out to sea to keep the different groups apart.

The segregation signs say either "Whites" or "Europeans." Now you may have thought that European meant someone who came from the continent of Europe, or whose ancestors came from there. That's only partly right. Among those who are considered European by the supporters of Apartheid are the Japanese.

Japan is still part of Asia as far as I know, and the authorities here look down their noses at Asians. But the Japanese are good business men and South Africa needs to do business with them; so the Japanese are officially classified as Europeans.

When you come to the Africans, you learn that the Apartheid people don't call them Africans. They may say natives—and I have seen a road sign like our cattle-crossing signs, saying WARNING—NATIVES CROSSING. On one of these signs some African with a sense of humour made a few changes, so that the sign said WARNING—NATIVES VERY CROSS.

Another Apartheid word for the Negro people is Bantu.

This is something like calling all Indians Iroquois, even though they might be Mohawks, Sioux, or Blackfeet. The nastier white-supremacy people call the Africans Kaffirs.

There has scarcely been a day since I have been here that some South African white man has not tried to convince me that all Africans are savages. They really believe this. Now the finest man I have met here is a Zulu chief named Albert Luthuli. He is in jail now because he is president of the African National Congress. Chief Luthuli is a very dignified man in his sixties, who dresses like the school-teacher that he used to be. Yet the Apartheid fanatics try to tell me that he is nothing but a savage and that he is ready to dress up in feathers, grab a spear, and chase all the white people out of the country.

You often say that adults don't understand teen-agers; here the root of all the trouble is that the white people don't understand Africans. The white people won't admit there are people like Chief Luthuli—and there are many Africans like him—who are as civilized as the whites. And the Government refuses even to discuss the country's problems with the Africans.

I have heard the Prime Minister, Dr. Verwoerd, declare he is a Christian and has a conscience; and I have watched him in Parliament, sitting calmly while his policemen dash around the city beating up every African they run into. It's a very strange brand of Christianity.

You know that it was the police shooting seventy Africans at a place called Sharpeville that brought me out here. The cemetery in which those people are buried has more graves of children than adults, because so many children die of gastro-enteritis and pneumonia. Of every thousand African babies born, only between seven and eight hundred survive to their second year. Only fifty-five out of every hundred Africans ever reach the age of sixteen. Malnutrition is common; the African people cannot make enough money to survive, and live on an average twenty years less than white people.

My lunch today cost about three dollars. That is more than two days' wages for an average African working in the cities. The Africans who have to work on the farms make less. Last year the average earnings in a month for a farm family of six to seven were only $25.

The first problem to be solved, the Bishop of Johannesburg told me, was decent wages for the Africans. Their wages are terribly low, but they have to pay just as much for groceries as the white people.

Because of the low wages, nearly every white family can employ one or more servants. The other day I met a girl named Della, who is a cousin of your friend Nicola in London. You are all about the same age. There is one difference: Della has never had to wash dishes or make beds. There is a servant to do it for her.

You may be the world champion at getting out of washing dishes and making beds; but such experience as you have had I don't think has done you any harm. What happens in a country like South Africa, where there are low-paid servants, is that the idea of superiority gets around. People look down on the Africans or the Coloured people who have to do the dirty work.

I wouldn't say that this was so in Della's case. She is pretty sensible. But a majority of the white South Africans feel they are really superior to black people, who have to do menial jobs in order to live. That's the way about 90 per cent of the white people of South Africa feel.

They will tell you how kind they are to the Africans, but they won't admit the African is a human being with hopes and ambitions. That's where you have to make a start against Apartheid—by convincing these people that there will never be any happiness in South Africa until all those who live here, whatever their colour, can live decent, happy lives.

Love,
Dad

6. THE ANGRY YOUNG MEN

FEW WHITE PEOPLE trouble to attend the dreary proceedings of the Treason Trial in the Pretoria synagogue. However, there is usually a fair attendance of Africans filling their side of the segregated gallery seats.

One day last March Chief Luthuli was summing up the aims of the African National Congress. "We do not hate the white man," he testified, "we hate only the system." No sooner had he spoken than from the African side of the spectators' benches came a short, mocking laugh.

The judges frowned and an angry court attendant started in search of the interruption. A cloud seemed to pass over the noble features of the chief. He knew that the sound of derision came from one of his own people.

Spurned by the white racialists, Chief Luthuli now bears another cross, the scorn of race-conscious Africans whose cry is "Africa for the Africans" and who have replaced the moderation of the African National Congress with a new militancy of their own. They have formed the Pan-Africanist National Congress, borrowing most of the A.N.C. goals of human and political rights but demanding they be granted by 1963.

"We stand for government of the African, by the African, for the African, with everybody owing his allegiance to Africa and prepared also to accept the rule of the African majority." This is the creed of the Pan-Africanists.

Their anthem is:

> We the black people
> Are crying out for our land
> Which was taken by crooks.
> They should leave it alone,
> They should leave it alone.

Robert Mangaliso (which means "wonderful") Sobukwe is the leader of the Pan-Africanists. He is thirty-five and his closest followers are like him, angry young men. Sobukwe's square-jawed determination is as typical of his outlook as Luthuli's patient countenance is symbolic of the older generation's long-suffering.

Sobukwe broke with the A.N.C. two years ago on the issue of militancy. He accused Luthuli of being too careful, too much under white influence, and too bourgeois. He chose as his idols Nkrumah of Ghana, Mboya of Kenya, Nyere of Tanganyika, and Banda of Nyasaland—all men of the new Africa who were proving the African could go it alone. He declared his intention to defy the law and to go to jail. Once in prison, he would accept no bail, no defence counsel, no fine.

To demonstrate the courage of his convictions, Sobukwe gave up his comfortable job as a lecturer in Bantu languages to the white students of Witwatersrand University. He gave the movement a new salute to replace the old congress thumbs-up sign, with the cry of "Afrika"; the Pan-Africanists hold up an outstretched hand and shout *"Izwe lethu* (Our land)." Next he prepared for martyrdom.

The first objective was to be the *dompass,* the "accursed" reference book that every African must carry. This was something every African suffered from and understood, and the

Pan-Africanists promised them action. This was bread-and-butter politics.

Sobukwe issued this proclamation:

> Sons and daughters of the soil, on Monday, March 21, 1960, we launch our Positive Decisive Action against the Pass Laws. Exactly 7 A.M. we launch. Oh yes, we launch —there is no doubt about it.
>
> We have reached the crossroads—we have crossed our historical Rubicon!
>
> At this stage of our struggle we have a choice before us. Are we still prepared to be half-human beings in our fatherland or are we prepared to be citizens—men and women in a democratic non-racial South Africa? How long shall we be called Bantu, Native, Non-European, Non-White, or Black, stinking Kaffir in our own fatherland.
>
> When shall be be called sir, Mr., Mrs., Miss, ladies and gentlemen? How long shall we stay in the squalors of Windermere, of the Sahara Desert of Nyanga West? How long shall we rot physically, spiritually and morally?
>
> How long shall we starve amid plenty in our fatherland? How long shall we be a rightless, voteless and voiceless 11,000,000 in our fatherland? On what meat doth this our Oppressive-White Man Boss feed that he has grown so great? Sons and daughters of Africa—there is a choice before us. We are either slaves or free men— that's all.
>
> Let the world take note, that we are not fighting Dr. Verwoerd, simply because he is Dr. Verwoerd; we are not fighting against the Nationalist Party or the United Party. We are not fighting against Europeans or Indians or Chinese.
>
> In short, we are fighting against nobody. Our energies and forces are directed against a set-up, against a conception and a myth. This myth: others call it racial

superiority, others call it *herrenvolk*-ism, others white leadership with justice, or white supremacy.

We are fighting against Calvinistic doctrine that a certain nation was specially chosen by God to lead, guide and protect other nations. This is our fight.

In order to destroy this myth of race superiority, the Pan-Africanist Congress has drawn up an unfolding program—which starts tomorrow and ends up in 1963 with the realization of the United States of Africa. We start with the Pass Laws, then the next thing and the next—up to 1963.

Very soon now we shall be launching. The step we are taking is historical, pregnant with untold possibilities. We must, therefore, appreciate our role. We must appreciate our responsibility.

The African people have entrusted their entire future to us. And we have sworn that we are leading them not to death, but to the life abundant.

My instructions, therefore, are that our people must be taught NOW and CONTINUOUSLY THAT IN THIS CAMPAIGN we are going to observe ABSOLUTE NON-VIOLENCE.

There are those in our own ranks who will be speaking irresponsibly of bloodshed and violence. They must be firmly told what our stand is.

Let us consider for a moment what violence will achieve. I say quite POSITIVELY, without fear of contradiction, that the only people who will benefit from violence are the Government and the police.

This is not a game. We are not gambling. We are taking our first step in the march to African independence and the United States of Africa. And we are not leading corpses to the new Africa. We are leading the vital, breathing and dynamic youth of our land. We are leading that youth, NOT TO DEATH, BUT TO THE LIFE ABUNDANT. Let us get that clear.

We are not going to fight or attempt to fight, insult or

attempt to insult, provoke or attempt to provoke the police in their lawful duties.

Any person who does shall be dealt with by the police, of course, and we, as an organization, shall further deal with him.

The same applies to the police. We do not want to be provoked in any manner.

Fellow Africans, the hour for service, sacrifice, and suffering has come. Let us march in unison to the United States of Africa. Let us march to a new and independent Africa.

Forward to independence!

This was the Pan-Africanist charter. In March, when it was written, Sobukwe claimed thirty thousand members for his movement. Each paid thirty-five cents to join and monthly dues of fourteen cents. Sobukwe toured the country and returned to Johannesburg claiming, "The Cape is *ours.*" Entire A.N.C. branches—office furniture, funds and all—were said to be joining the P.A.C. Someone reminded Sobukwe of the South African slogan "Whether in business or politics, a man or a movement is made or broken on the Rand." He replied confidently, "The Rand is ours as well."

Sobukwe told the story of an old man in the Johannesburg Negro suburb of Orlando East. When P.A.C. organizers called on him, the elderly African said: "I have been a member of the A.N.C. for most of my life. But go inside. Take my son."

The Pan-Africanists promised *action.* "We will send our leaders to jail first," they promised. "That is where our leaders belong—in front."

About the whites, Sobukwe might say, "We are not against them, we are just against the system"; but his followers made clear they considered the white people a "foreign minority."

Only the Negro and the mulatto were considered by the

Pan-Africanists to have basic rights in South Africa. Unlike Luthuli and the A.N.C., which co-operated with congresses of all races, the P.A.C. refused to have anything to do with the Indians.

"It pays the big Indian merchants to have things as they are," Sobukwe said, "although I don't dispute that they might be interested in more rights for themselves. But 'Damn the African,' as far as they are concerned. They are not one with us; but if the Indian working class, which is oppressed just like us, threw up its own leadership, then we could work with them. But at present, we can't work with the Indians. Not with their present leaders."

Introducing Sobukwe to its readers, the magazine *Drum* explained how he had given up his teaching job and how "this means that he's also given up bacon and eggs for breakfast every day, and a car for life as well as the chance to move freely in white liberal society."

Sobukwe himself explained his renunciation of the academic life by telling the story of two wolves who lived in a forest. The one wolf was lean and hungry, the other fat and contented.

> One day the fat wolf said to the thin wolf: "Look, why don't you come and stay with me. My master feeds me well as you can see, and he'll give you room and food." It sounded a good idea, and the thin wolf walked along with the fat wolf for a while. Then he noticed that there was something tied around the fat wolf's neck.
> He stopped and asked the fat wolf: "What's that?"
> And the fat wolf said: "This thing? Oh, that's nothing."
> "Come on, come on," said the thin wolf. "What is that?"
> "Well," said the fat wolf, "that's a collar. You see, my master ties me up at night."

"In that case, I won't go with you. I'd rather be free, even if I must stay hungry," said the thin wolf.

"The Africanists are like the thin wolf," said Sobukwe.

On Friday, March 18, Sobukwe announced the P.A.C. anti-pass campaign would open the following Monday. With Pan-Africanists at their head, crowds of Africans were to march to the nearest police station and demand to be arrested for not carrying their passes. The jails were to be filled, the courts overloaded, while businesses and factories would come to a standstill without African labour.

True to his word, Sobukwe and his national secretary, the fiery little Potlako Leballo ("We believe in only one race—the human race.") led a group of sixty "resistors" to the police station in Orlando township and demanded to be detained for violating the pass laws. It was a small demonstration and the police were happy to oblige them.

A thousand miles away at Cape Town, the two locations of Langa and Nyanga were better organized. The crowd of demonstrators numbered in the thousands. The police refused to accede to their demand for arrest, and before nightfall three people had been shot to death.

At Sharpeville, thirty miles from Johannesburg, the South African police completely lost control of themselves and presented the Pan-Africanist Congress with its first martyrs.

Chief Luthuli issued a dignified call in the name of the African National Congress for a national Day of Mourning to be held one week later, Monday, March 28.

From his cell in Johannesburg, Sobukwe went the chief one further. He called on his followers not only to stay away from work on the Day of Mourning but to remain home for the remainder of the week.

"The struggle continues," Sobukwe declared in a message smuggled out of jail. "The best way to mourn your dead is to join the campaign in which they died. Come to jail where they were going. Come in your hundreds of thousands."

Sobukwe's statement was handed to me in a shabby little Johannesburg office rented by a struggling African trade union. The man who passed it on was twenty-four-year-old William Jolobe, a P.A.C. spokesman who, by that time, five days after Sharpeville, was one of the movement's few officers to have escaped arrest.

Jolobe was a small, earnest man with a troubled face. It was something of a shock to hear him telling me, "I don't hate a white man automatically just because of the colour of his skin." In painstaking English he outlined for me the history and aims of the P.A.C. and explained some of their techniques.

He said Sobukwe was national president but had trained an understudy who had been ready to take over when the leader went to jail. In each of their regional organizations the same method was employed—a trained substitute for every executive. And the first duty of the substitute when he took over was to begin training his own replacement. Later, I was to see this technique in action near Cape Town, where the P.A.C. was most highly organized. In the course of a week the P.A.C. produced and the police arrested six tiers of leadership.

Immediately after Sharpeville, Dr. Verwoerd had banned all public meetings; but on Saturday, March 26, he made an exception for himself by holding a gathering of Nationalists at Meyerton. The site was less than a dozen miles from Sharpeville and the premier's choice of time and place for a rally of racialists seemed provocative.

Jolobe said it had been considered by the P.A.C. whether to

demonstrate at the Verwoerd meeting, but a decision had been reached against any action. They would conserve their forces for the Day of Mourning and attempt to extend it into an indefinite stay-at-home strike.

Into this situation stepped the Union of South Africa's national police chief, Major-General C. I. Rademeyer. Just before the prime minister was to speak at Meyerton, Gen. Rademeyer made an astounding announcement: there would be no more pass arrests for the time being.

Gen. Rademeyer's statement explained:

> In view of the fact that Bantus as a result of intimidation, are so gripped by fear to carry reference books or other documents, and are even afraid to carry money, I have decided to relieve this tremendous tension and to prevent innocent and law-abiding Bantus from landing in trouble.
>
> I have instructed that no Bantu, male or female, is to be asked for his or her reference book or any other document.
>
> No Bantu will be taken into custody because he is not in possession of his reference book.
>
> Bantus must not be arrested and detained for all sorts of petty offences. They must be warned or summoned to appear.

The police chief's announcement was a complete reversal of Prime Minister Verwoerd's pronouncement that there would be no concessions. The country's senior police official flatly ordered his men to disobey a law, albeit one that occupied a third of their time. It was also a law that for thirty years had been the underlying cause of African unrest.

Was this the first crack in the fortress of Apartheid? Was it a liberal gesture, or a tactical move acknowledging that the police were not in a position to carry out the law? Why was the announcement made by a police officer, and not by the Prime Minister or one of his Cabinet?

In the first flush of excitement following the dramatic announcement, it was suggested that this marked the end of the pass system; that no longer would Africans be summarily arrested and "sold" to farmers as cheap labour, and that the pass would no longer be a badge of shame.

It proved to be a tactical move. The pass laws in all their iniquity were soon to be reimposed. First to see the emptiness of Gen. Rademeyer's "concession" was Chief Luthuli. In the political bargaining for African support between the African National Congress and the Pan-Africanist Congress, it was his move. He had called the Day of Mourning only to be outbid by Sobukwe, who wanted a Week of Mourning. Now it was the A.N.C.'s turn.

Chief Luthuli publicly burned his pass. A picture of him doing so appeared in the Johannesburg *Sunday Times* (almost causing suppression of the paper for incitement). In the African locations hundreds of Luthuli's followers imitated his example, but not the half million he had hoped for.

Sobukwe, in a jail interview, could only reply, "I am not impressed with the burning of passes and I declare again that there should be no violence in our campaign. But I have no objection to any African organization which joins our fight against passes."

The mass of the country's African population failed to follow either leader. The pass system had become so much a part of their lives that they could not conceive of life without passes, and they did not answer the call of defiance. Their bewildered attitude showed they were not yet ready to throw off their chains.

Only outside Cape Town, at Langa and Nyanga, did the

Pan-Africanist resistance hold out past the Day of Mourning.

As they went from house to house, the A.N.C. organizers trying to find fuel for a bonfire of passes realized the average African's attachment to these marks of bondage. Without them they could not apply for a house, draw an old-age pension, or deposit their savings. They had been conditioned to living with a pass. Like the ancient prisoner who accidentally found the prison gates ajar, they could not be persuaded to leave the security of their bondage.

The Pan-Africanists saw this and switched their campaign away from burning passes to trying to persuade their followers that they could indeed live without having to carry a pass.

Some wondered why the Pan-Africanists had been allowed to organize to the point where they could stage the demonstrations at Sharpeville and outside Cape Town. "Was it," asked London's *Daily Telegraph*, "because it is easier to send armoured cars round the native townships of Johannesburg than to answer Chief Luthuli, the Congress's rusticated President, when he tells his white fellow-citizens: 'We do not want to kick you out of the country and we do not want to marry your sisters: all we want is a fair deal in our own country.' One is left with the suspicion that it is the moderate Africans whom the Union Government most fear and that the kind of demonstration that can be dealt with by diving Sabre jets is not altogether unwelcome to them."

Two days after the Day of National Mourning, Chief Luthuli was back in jail as the Government attempted to round up every African leader. In the leaderless townships and locations, Africans debated whether to follow Sobukwe or Luthuli. The best that the liberal whites could hope for was that if Chief Luthuli were released he might still command a following and be able to negotiate grievances with a tolerant administration—if it could be found.

A third candidate for African leadership might be somewhere among the temporarily submissive nine million-odd Africans. Should he emerge, the question of whether militant Sobukwe might supplant moderate Luthuli would become academic. There was every chance that the new leader might be more reckless than either of the imprisoned Congress leaders.

7. *DRUM*

TO FIND OUT what was happening in South Africa, one of the first things I did on my arrival in Johannesburg was to buy a copy of a magazine for Africans called *Drum*. This was three days after Sharpeville, the first major demonstration by the Pan-Africanists. *Drum* did not disappoint me. Across a full-colour cover shot of Mamsie Mthombeni, a grinning girl in pedal pushers, there was a label: WHO ARE THE AFRICANISTS? Inside, the lead article provided the answer under the title FIREWORKS—OR FALSE-ALARM?

This was a magazine scoop—as if the Democratic nomination for president had been won by an unknown and the *Saturday Evening Post,* planned, written, and edited weeks in advance, had appeared the same day with a profile of the dark-horse candidate.

Drum bills itself as "Africa's leading magazine," and this is a modest claim. With only minute financial resources, it has earned its way into the same category as *Life* and *Paris-Match*—picture magazines with a flair. Indeed, *Life's* pictures of Sharpeville were taken by *Drum* photographers. If anything, *Drum* has the edge on its wealthy rivals because of its crusading spirit. Among writers, editors, and photographers *Drum* is one of those papers one dreams of joining and, of course, never does.

A brilliant magazine man who made reality of this dream

was Tom Hopkinson, *Drum*'s editor since 1958. He had been editor of the outstanding English publication, *Picture Post*, until he staked his job on an issue of principle and resigned. (The issue was an article by one of his writers, James Cameron, on the "gook" attitude of U.S. and Commonwealth troops during the Korean War. Hopkinson wanted to publish the facts; his employer said the article would harm the war effort.) Not long after, Hopkinson had the bitter satisfaction of seeing his successors turn *Picture Post* into a purveyor of cheesecake, a policy that led to its decline and disappearance.

When I visited Hopkinson in his Johannesburg office, he was revelling in his work. "This is the key moment and this is the key place," he declared, his pale blue eyes lighting up. "There are two great problems in the world today—East versus West, and Black versus White. The problems of Black and White are centred in Johannesburg. There have to be gigantic social changes here. As a journalist in South Africa I can help people; as a human being, I have the satisfaction of feeling that I am making some contribution in trying to solve the situation."

Hopkinson worked with a staff of six, half white and half African, putting out a ninety-four-page monthly magazine. In addition he had one-man bureaus in each of the Union's principal cities; but it was a miniscule organization for a magazine that was not only selling throughout South Africa but which produced special editions for East and West African countries.

Drum's Ghana edition alone sold 60,000 copies, and it was a blow to the enterprise when Prime Minister Nkrumah reacted to the South African crisis by banning *Drum* on the grounds that it was subject to the censorship of white racialists.

The magazine is owned by whites. It was founded in 1951 and its publisher was James Bailey, the son of the Johannesburg gold millionaire, Sir Abe Bailey. When his father died, Bailey, a Battle of Britain pilot and an Oxford graduate, took over the family flock of 4,000 sheep and their race-horse stud. The magazine began as *African Drum,* an almost cultural publication featuring articles on music of the tribes, the history of Bantu tribes, and instalments of Alan Paton's best seller, *Cry, the Beloved Country.*

The Government welcomed this innocuous magazine and sent copies of it abroad as examples of Bantu achievement under Apartheid. Africans were not so enthusiastic; the circulation was twenty thousand and Bailey was losing $5,600 a month. He sent to England for a young man he had known at Oxford, Anthony Sampson.

Sampson was not a professional journalist, but under his editorship *Drum* found its formula. With Bailey, he went around talking to Africans about the magazine. One of them was Job Rathebe, a suave undertaker and boxing promoter. "I can tell you what's wrong with *Drum,*" Rathebe said. "You see, it's got the white hand on it—that's what I call it. *Drum* is what white men want Africans to be, not what they are.

"Now, take this tribal-history business, which you call 'Know Yourselves.' We all know ourselves quite well enough, Mr. Bailey, I assure you. And we're trying to get away from our tribal history as fast as we can. We don't want *Drum* to remind us. What we want, you see, is a paper that belongs to us—a real black paper. We want it to be our *Drum,* not a white man's *Drum.*"

Sampson and Bailey began to swing away from preaching tribal culture and folk tales. They appointed an African editorial board to advise on policy and switched to a straight commercial mixture of girls, crime, animals, and babies. Circulation rose to 35,000, but this was less than a rival picture magazine for Africans called *Zonk*. What was more depressing to the staff was the fact that *Drum* was regarded with suspicion by the Africans. Some said it was backed by the Chamber of Mines, others that it was a Colonial Office propaganda sheet. Sampson shrewdly decided that *Drum* needed to show that it was for, and not against, its readers.

Drum's sports editor was a jaunty young African named Henry Nxumalo. He had an enthusiastic, intelligent face—high forehead, prominent cheekbones, and a wide, strong mouth always ready to burst into a grin. Nxumalo's grandfather had been a tribal Zulu with three wives; his father had died while Henry was at school, and he had run away—first to Durban, and then to Johannesburg, where he worked for seven dollars a month in a boilermaker's shop and wrote poetry in his spare time.

The war gave Nxumalo an opportunity to see the outside world. He joined the army as a camp follower—Africans were not allowed to bear arms in the South African army—and was posted to Cairo, then to England. In London he mixed with African and white intellectuals. This was a little too much for the South African army. He was shipped home and discharged. After leaving the army, he got a job as a sports writer and joined *Drum*.

One day Nxumalo asked Sampson whether he had heard of a place called Bethel. "It's a farming district in the Eastern Transvaal, where they grow potatoes. Of course, there's a good deal of flogging goes on there."

Sampson sensed the story possibilities and called for the file of newspaper clippings. They went back to 1929, when a Bethel farmer was found guilty of tying an African labourer by his feet from a tree, pouring scalding water into his mouth when he cried out for something to drink, and ending his agony by flogging him to death.

The clippings were a record of brutality—beatings, whippings, setting dogs on Africans, and murder. Bethel, which means "House of God," was a living hell for African farm labourers, many of them shanghaied into working as almost slaves. Some signed contracts to work at Bethel as an alternative to going to jail for breaking the pass laws. Others were convicts hired out by farmers from the Government.

Henry Nxumalo volunteered to visit Bethel and research a story for *Drum*. He discarded his dapper city outfit and went there in rags like a farm labourer. Two days later he called Sampson and asked that *Drum*'s white photographer, Jurgen Schadeberg, join him. They visited eight different farms and talked to about fifty labourers. Of the fifty, not one was satisfied with conditions, and thirty-two said they had been tricked into signing contracts.

Schadeberg's pictures confirmed Nxumalo's story. They showed labourers eating dry porridge off filthy sacks, and boss-boys on horseback, armed with long whips, driving the gangs of potato pickers. By various ruses he also managed to get shots of the high-walled compounds with their barbed-wire fencing and, inside, the bare rooms with concrete ledges for beds.

Only one thing was lacking—direct evidence of the way in which the labourers were recruited. Nxumalo offered to get himself hired to work at Bethel. He went to the Johannesburg Pass Office, where Africans line up each day to get passes that will allow them to stay in the city and look for work.

Nxumalo waited until a sharply dressed African appeared and began trying to get people to sign up for farm work. (He was paid seventy cents a head for those he recruited.) Nxumalo told the man he was in trouble without a pass, and the recruiter said he could get him work. They went together to an employment agency run by a white man.

The reporter spent the night in a filthy compound with scores of Africans without passes. The next morning fifty of them were lined up and the terms of the contract read to them. They were to work for six months for $8.40 a month plus food and quarters. They were to be given an advance of seventy cents pocket money, $1.45 for food, and $2.00 train fare. This was to be deducted from their first month's wages.

The signing was accomplished by the government attesting officer holding a pencil over the contract and the fifty men running past him, each touching the pencil. Nxumalo refused to "touch the pencil" and managed to escape with a copy of the contract.

Drum came out with a report, "Bethel Today." The story appeared under the by-line "Mr. Drum" and was to become the first of a series of exposures. *Drum* had found its formula and had won the confidence of its African readers.

There was no lack of material for Mr. Drum. He visited the Cape vineyards where Negro and mulatto workers, including children, were paid part of their wages in wine under the "tot system" and, as a result, spent much of their time stupefied.

The sugar farms of Natal also received Mr. Drum's attention. There he found Indian children who had worked an eight-hour day for seven cents, and adult workers virtually enslaved, working vainly to pay off debts to their employers.

Circulation rose under the new policy, and within a year

of Mr. Drum's debut at Bethel the magazine was selling 60,000 copies a month.

Drum itself was subject to the laws of Apartheid. If an African reporter went out on an assignment with a white photographer, they would have to take separate taxis, one driven by a white man and the other, second class, run by a Negro. White and black staff men could never travel in the same train or bus, eat together in a restaurant, or be together in a theatre or a park.

The same laws applied to the magazine's contents. No pictures of white starlets—they might excite African lusts. Marilyn Monroe's charms will never be displayed in *Drum,* but the laws of racial supremacy do not object to Negro readers seeing France Nuyen or other half-caste beauties. One sly *Drum* feature recently showed a beautiful Zulu girl, Doreen Madombo, strolling the streets of Cape Town clad in tight slacks and a halter top. The photographer cleverly included the leering looks of the white people who watched her pass.

Objections were made when *Drum* printed a photo showing Mrs. Eleanor Roosevelt shaking hands with a Negro woman, Mrs. Edith Sampson. It was forbidden for the magazine to print shots of Negro boxers in the ring with white opponents. According to the racialists, that would constitute "incitement."

Drum's readers demanded a full ration of crime stories. I noticed Hopkinson skip over one called "I Drove for the Payroll Bandits" as he leafed through the files with me. He explained that the biggest readership was for African success stories—a profile of a garage owner who now owned a Cadillac. "Their lives are so full of misery that they don't want to read about it in a magazine," Hopkinson explained.

With a quarter million Africans going to jail every year, *Drum* had to study the prison system. One debasing aspect was the "Tausa dance" that prisoners were forced to perform naked while wardens searched their clothes for contraband. This was a daily rite that I was to watch in disgust while a prisoner at Durban.

African work parties were sent out of the jails each morning to clean up streets and parks. On their return they were obliged to remove their canvas shorts and red T-shirts. While nude, they had to execute a jig step, hands over heads, to show nothing was hidden on their persons.

Drum's problem was how to get photographs. Sampson discovered that the Johannesburg jail, the Fort, was overlooked by a nurses' residence. From the roof of this building it was possible to look down into the prison yard. Enlisting the aid of his secretary, Deborah Duncan, he armed her with a small camera and sent her to ask the superintendent of nurses for permission to photograph the view of Johannesburg from the residence roof.

With Miss Duncan, disguised as her "boys," went two of *Drum*'s African photographers. They were armed with a camera with a telescopic lens. While Miss Duncan snapped the view and held the superintendent's attention, the "boys" focussed on the prison yard and the naked inmates going through their humiliating dance.

They got their picture, published it, and secured a temporary halt to the "Tausa dance" custom. The angered Government retaliated by adding another law to the statute books. In future no one might photograph or describe jail life in South Africa.

Before the new law came into effect, Mr. Drum had been to jail himself. It proved a difficult story to arrange. Henry

Nxumalo had become so popular as Mr. Drum that he found it difficult to get himself arrested. He arranged to enter a location without a permit and let the police know about it. They sent him away with the admonition not to do it again.

Nxumalo then refused to pay his fare on a train. When the case came up in court the arresting officer failed to appear and the magistrate dismissed the case. He picketted Marshall Square, Johannesburg's main police station, with a bottle of brandy sticking out of his pocket. No one paid him any attention.

He drank the brandy in front of the police station without getting any attention. Only when he felt its effects and got involved in a brawl was he lodged in the cells. The next day he appeared in court on a charge of drunkenness.

"Five days or five shillings," sang out the magistrate. Mr. Drum turned to go down to the cells, satisfied that he had achieved his aim of a minimum sentence. The court interpreter intervened. "It's all right, Henry," he told him, "I've paid your fine. You're free."

Finally, an African constable arrested Henry for breaking the curfew. He was given five days and served four, with one day off for good conduct. His report, "Mr. Drum Goes to Jail," revealed that he had been kicked or thrashed every day. He exposed food conditions—breakfast of yellow porridge with half-cooked pieces of turnips, carrots, and other vegetables. No spoons were provided and the meal had to be eaten with soiled hands he had not been allowed to wash after emptying latrine buckets.

Henry Nxumalo continued his muck-raking career as Mr. Drum, until one night in 1956 he failed to return from an assignment. He had been knifed to death by an African gangster. His murder was a mystery until a confession was received by the police stating that the writer had been paid to kill Nxumalo. A man was arrested, who disavowed the confession but was found guilty of the killing. No satisfactory motive for the crime was ever made clear.

Drum continued its exposure of shameful conditions. A feature on Durban showed how 355 out of every thousand African babies born there die before the age of six. Most of them could be saved by a free-milk scheme costing a nickel a day. "That caused a bit of a stir," said Hopkinson.

Instead of acting to prevent starvation, Durban boasts of its fine hospital for non-Europeans. It is a very good, if over-crowded, hospital where cases of malnutrition are cured, only to return to the identical conditions that caused them.

"How White Are the Whites?" asked another *Drum* series in which archivist Kathleen Jeffreys, a white woman with a small shop opposite the Parliament buildings in Cape Town, declared, "No one in South Africa should be ashamed of his colour. And for the white man it is almost proof of long citizenship to have a touch of colour."

The articles were accompanied by a chart showing that any white family that had been established in South Africa for six generations most probably included some coloured blood. The climax of Miss Jeffreys' research was the suggestion that the grand old Boer, President Oom Paul Kruger, himself had a non-white ancestor in his family tree.

Miss Jeffreys was able to show that in the early days of the Cape settlement fifteen to thirty of the marriages were mixed, and that it was not until 1857 that the Dutch Reformed Church began drawing the colour line that it now defends as divinely inspired.

Another *Drum* article, lighter in vein, showed how mulattoes crossed the colour line and passed as whites. In Cape

Town, Apartheid made it an offence for Africans to attend movie theatres designated for Coloured audiences. *Drum* pointed out that this left the Negroes with only open-air shows, and got the regulation reversed.

When the Government banished an African trade-union leader, Mrs. E. Mafeking, to the Zulu bush, separating her from her husband and family by eight hundred miles, *Drum* was the first to find her and tell her story. Mrs. Mafeking, in defiance of the banishment order, which would have confined her to an area where she could be employed only at housework, had escaped into the British enclave of Basutoland.

The white Government has the power to banish Africans without their having a chance to appeal, and more than eighty people have been exiled. *Drum* discovered that some had been driven into mental illness by this cruel punishment, and told the story of a banished woman who feared to be left alone. "The light," she said, "has gone out of my day."

The contacts of the African staff members have made it possible for *Drum* to anticipate political developments. The magazine's first article about the Pan-Africanist leader Sobukwe carried with it an explanation for the readers showing who this coming man was. The article on the Pan-Africanists that appeared at the time of the Sharpeville massacre was a superb piece of editorial judgment and timing. The price *Drum* paid, three or four weeks later, was to have the police raid its offices and seize all available copies of the issue that had not yet been sold.

The first thing that strikes a visitor entering the *Drum* editorial offices on Johannesburg's Troye Street is a sign over Tom Hopkinson's name. It says MY HOME NUMBER IS . . . . THE NUMBER OF OUR LAWYER IS . . . .

The notice is the visible evidence of the censorship under which all South African editors live. Under the Emergency Regulations imposed on March 30, the Minister of Justice can close down any newspaper, prohibit the printing, publication, or dissemination of any matter, and suppress all news.

Under the Criminal Law Amendment Act of 1953 (which has been in force ever since):

> Any person who . . . uses any language or does any act or thing calculated to cause any person or persons in general to commit an offence by way of protest against a law or in support of any campaign against the law or in support of any campaign for the repeal or modification of any law or the variation or limitation of the application or administration of any law shall be guilty of an offence and liable upon conviction to:
>
>   i. a fine not exceeding $1,680; or
>   ii. imprisonment not exceeding five years; or
>   iii. a whipping not exceeding ten strokes; or
>   iv. both such fine and such imprisonment; or
>   v. both such fine and such whipping; or
>   vi. both such imprisonment and such a whipping.
>
> Provided that in the case of a second or subsequent conviction it shall not be competent to impose a fine except in conjunction with whipping or imprisonment.

Editing a newspaper or magazine under these conditions, observed the editor of the Johannesburg *Star,* "is like walking blindfold through a mine field."

Not satisfied with these powers, the Government introduced at the 1960 session of Parliament a Publications and Entertainments Bill to control publication of newspapers, periodicals, books, films, and recordings. Ostensibly designed to protect the public from indecent or offensive matter, the bill does not confine itself to morals but includes political views.

As in all legislation affecting publications, the catch comes in the definition of what is "offensive". According to the Nationalist Government Bill, a publication will be deemed to be undesirable if it endangers the safety of the State, has the effect of disturbing the peace and good order, or is detrimental to the general welfare.

These definitions are wide enough to give the Government an excuse to crack down on any publication that does not conform to the Nationalists' rigid moral and political views.

Other grounds for declaring a publication undesirable are that it offends decency (no definition of decency provided), that it offends the religious convictions and feelings of any section of the population, that it is detrimental to relations between any section of the population, or that it promotes crime.

The Cronje Commission of Enquiry in regard to Undesirable Publications recommended that a law be passed banning advertisements showing ladies in their underwear, and ruled dangerous any printed matter "deemed indecent, offensive or harmful by the ordinary civilized, decent, reasonable and responsible inhabitants of the Union".

Where these "ordinary civilized, decent, reasonable and responsible inhabitants" will come from will be out of the ranks of the most bigoted. And their victims will be the liberals, like the editors of *Drum*, who have tried to form a bridge between white and black.

"The ignorance of white South Africans about the black," Hopkinson told me, "cannot be believed. It is like Britain in

Dickens' time, when the English middle class was in total darkness about the conditions of the working classes.

"Even well-meaning whites not hostile to the African will ask me, 'Do you discuss things with your African staff? What happens if they disagree with you?'

"One of the things that is most significant is that, while there has always been a term of hostility or contempt among the whites for the white man who tries to maintain contact with the black—in Afrikaans it's *Kaffirboetie*—in the last couple of years the Africans have invented a name of hostility for their people who mix with white people. The word is 'sell-out,' and it's being used more often now, when the need for contact is greater than ever."

8. FARMS

IT WAS A *Drum* photographer who told me one of the most chilling stories I heard in South Africa, and showed me the photographs authenticating it. He had been on an assignment near Weenen, about 150 miles from Durban, when one of the local residents asked, "Have you seen our hospital?" The man would say no more, but urged the photographer to see for himself.

The hospital, a fifty- or sixty-bed building, was in charge of an African matron who was doing her utmost to cope with about two hundred patients. Most of the cases were either malnutrition or tuberculosis.

It is common, even in the big King Edward hospital for non-Europeans in Durban, for three and four African children, suffering from semi-starvation, to be kept in one cot. At the hospital near Weenen few of the children were lucky enough to have cots. They slept under the beds, on the floor, or cradled in their mothers' arms. One dormitory had no beds at all.

The photographs were sickening. The horror was heightened by the mothers' efforts to smile for the camera. One lies stretched out on the floor cuddling her youngsters.

The *Drum* man recorded the scenes inside this modern pest house, and on his way out of the district encountered a white woman. He asked her if she were aware of the over-crowded hospital.

"Oh, yes," she replied. "The amount of tuberculosis is frightening. We didn't realize it until our pigs became infected with t.b. They picked it up from the native herd boys."

About one-third (3,261,227) of the Africans live in what are considered the white rural areas of South Africa. Another 3,651,830 live in African areas, and 2,622,872 in the urban districts (South African Bureau of Census and Statistics, 1957).

Large numbers of white South African farmers have heeded government warnings to use African labour more efficiently on their farms, and to maintain acceptable standards and conditions of work for their help. But the country's agriculture is disgraced in some districts where Africans work under semi-slavery.

Influx control limiting the entry of Africans to the cities virtually forces the African farm labourer to remain on the land. His wages are also kept at an artificially low level by government action. (During the 1960 demonstrations, industrial and commercial interests expressed willingness to double urban wage scales from $1.40 a day to $2.80. The offer was rejected by the Government, largely out of fear of the effect on the rural worker.)

Drum's exposure of conditions at Bethel illustrates one method farmers use to obtain labour. This is the contract system, which is abused by serious underpayment, inadequate rations, and downright cruelty. According to the South African Institute of Race Relations, an independent academic body, which also investigated Bethel, in 20 per cent of the cases they studied African labourers suffered ill-treatment.

Improvements were made at Bethel, but the contract system is still used and still abused. A recent *Drum* inquiry, "We Call It Semi-Slavery," revealed cases of children of fourteen signed up as contract labourers. One of *Drum's* African photographers got inside the compound where the workers were housed, by pretending he wanted to buy food. He had to buy and eat the food—it nauseated him—as the price for getting his pictures.

Shots of bent-back labourers weeding a field under the supervision of an overseer were obtained by parking a car near a field where they worked. While Hopkinson pretended to be lost and asked directions of the overseer, one of his cameramen stole pictures from a rear window. "Those workers," Hopkinson recalled, "were working literally for dear life."

The *Sunday Times* of Johannesburg on September 27, 1959, reported a court case illustrating conditions on a farm owned by P. C. Beckenstrater in the White River district. The testimony showed that Beckenstrater recruited twenty-four Africans in May to work at a place called Louis Trichardt on thirty-day contracts.

Instead of being taken to the place named in the contract, they were transported to White River. The workers were then threatened that unless they would agree to longer contracts, they would get no food. Fifteen caved in and signed six-month contracts. The nine who refused were hauled into court for having failed to obey orders from Beckenstrater.

An African has little chance of justice where he is accused of breaking a contract or refusing a white man's orders. The nine Africans were sentenced to fourteen days imprisonment, sentence to be suspended if they returned to work. The nine stuck together and elected to go to jail.

After serving their time, the nine were then compelled to

report to Beckenstrater to complete the original thirty-day contract. According to the white farmer, this meant thirty full days—time spent in prison, time off due to illness, or days when weather made work impossible were not counted. The pay was $8.40 for the thirty days.

The story does not end here. Some of the Africans decided to take their case to the Native Commissioner, a white man charged with safeguarding African interests. On their way they were arrested and charged again with desertion. Once more they went to jail. This time they did desert, some of them not bothering to wait for their miserable pay. They were hauled into court again, but this time a magistrate refused to convict them.

Other unscrupulous farmers deduct from the wretched wages money for transporting contract labourers to and from the farms; some charge their victims exorbitant prices for clothing supplied—in many cases pieces of gunny sacking.

Brutality is usually traced to African boss-boys, overseers who for a few extra dollars are willing to beat or whip their fellow-men. But some white farmers are not above taking the law into their own hands. One of the most recent was the case of H. B. Pieterse, of the Heidelberg area, in August 1959. He beat one of his African labourers to death.

The charge was culpable homicide. Pieterse was found guilty. The sentence? Twelve months imprisonment.

The second system of obtaining farm labour cheaply is by using jail prisoners. In 1953-54 there were in South Africa a hundred thousand "convict volunteer labourers" on farms. The Government charged the farmers who used them ten cents a head per day.

The Government is most obliging. If a farmer builds a jail on his estate, the Government will staff it with guards and prisoners. In 1956 there were fifteen such farm jails, with an average daily population of 4,394.

Hiring prison labour to farmers was justified on these grounds:

1. It is common knowledge that large numbers of natives are daily being arrested and prosecuted for contraventions of a purely technical nature.

2. These arrests cost the State large sums of money and serve no useful purpose.

3. The Department of Justice, the South African Police and the Department for Native Affairs have therefore held consultations on the problem and have evolved a scheme, the object of which is to induce unemployed natives now roaming about the streets in the various urban areas to accept employment outside such urban areas.

4. This scheme aims primarily at assisting unemployed natives to obtain employment, but it is self-evident that one of its results will be that the number of unemployed natives in the urban areas will be greatly reduced and there would also be less temptation for such natives to resort to crime as a means of livelihood. (From an official circular issued by the Secretary for Native Affairs, June 14, 1954)

Everything is in the interests of the lowly savage. But this was not quite how this high-minded scheme worked in practice. Under the plan, Africans arrested for minor and purely technical offences were not charged immediately, but were escorted by police to a district labour bureau where they were offered rural employment. If they accepted, they were freed of impending charges.

The Chief Bantu Affairs Commissioner for the Witwatersrand reported that in 1958 the police hauled 14,154 petty offenders to the Johannesburg district labour bureau. Of these 2,337 were placed in employment, mainly on farms; 9,591 were returned to the police for prosecution; 1,084 were released because it was found they were genuinely employed; 24 went to hospital; 607 were deported as prohibited immigrants from outside the Union; 197 were released after paying taxes; and 314 deserted.

The South African Institute for Race Relations reported, "Alleged petty offenders who accepted work on farms were kept at the district labour bureaus until the farmers came to collect them, being afforded no opportunity of informing their relatives of their whereabouts, or of fetching clothes and money. Hundreds of African families suffered grave anxiety, and experienced many practical difficulties, when the breadwinners suddenly disappeared."

One African social worker explained the nature of these "practical difficulties." He had been asked to investigate the case of two teen-age children held on a charge of theft. Their mother was dead. Their father had been picked up as a petty offender. It took the social worker three months, with the assistance of government authorities, to find the father and reunite the family.

Some of the petty offenders feared they faced long prison terms if they turned down the farm jobs. In fact, the sentences for their alleged crimes would have been between $2.80 and $14.00, with the alternative of seven to thirty days in jail.

Others were under the impression that if they served their time on a farm, they could return to the city. If they did this they were open to re-arrest, and the same cycle of a choice between the police and the farm. More than three hundred deserted, although the farmers usually transported them in locked trucks and confiscated their pass books.

DT163.N45

DT846.K3m3

D196.3.P75

Title	Authors	ISBN
Respiration	Lambers, Hans; Ribas-Carbo,	978-1-4020-3588-
Tissue Culture Engineering	Dutta Gupta, S.; Ibaraki, Yasuomi	978-1-4020-3594-
-Associated Bacteria	Gnanamanickam, Samuel S.	978-1-4020-4536-
-ation Technology in Tropical Forest Science	Ishii, K.; Sakurai, S.; Sasaki, S.; Suzuki, K.	978-4-431-28053-
a Astrophysics, Part I	Somov, Boris V.	978-0-387-34916-
a Physics	Dinklage, Andreas; Klinger, Thomas; Marx, Gerrit; Schweikhard, Lutz	978-3-540-25274-
a Physics and Controlled Nuclear Fusion	Miyamoto, Kenro	978-3-540-24217-
a-Material Interaction in Controlled Fusion	Naujoks, D.	978-3-540-32148-
city and Signal Representation in the Auditory	Merzenich, Michael M.; Syka, Josef	978-0-387-23154-
ity in the Visual System	De Weerd, Peter; Pinaud, Raphael; Tremere, Liisa A.	978-0-387-28189-

Joel Carlson, a Johannesburg lawyer, investigated conditions under which some of the victims of this scheme worked. On at least four farms the labourers were locked up at nights to prevent them from escaping. They were kept in badly ventilated huts, where they had only filthy blankets or sacks infested with lice. Half-drums were used as sanitary pails; there was not enough water for washing, let alone drinking, and the food consisted mainly of cornmeal. It was stated in the report that on some farms the African straw bosses were paid a bonus based on the amount of work completed, and these boss-boys beat any labourer who appeared to be slacking.

Cornelius Mokgoko was a slow worker. He had been sent from Pretoria to the farm of R. C. Meiring in the Bethel district. He lasted three days, collapsing and dying in the fields without medical attention. At the inquest his fellow-workers said because Cornelius was slow Meiring and his boss-boys beat him unmercifully over the three days.

This "voluntary" scheme, Apartheid's considered solution to African unemployment, was so abused that in June 1959 the Government temporarily suspended it. But they maintained the equally abused system of renting out convict labour.

One of the excuses for the convict-labour system is that it helps keep minor offenders away from hardened criminals in South Africa's teeming jails. The prison authorities try to ensure that this system is not abused and can blacklist a farm where conditions are unsatisfactory.

Farmers can get convict labour in a number of ways. Medium-term prisoners may be sent to jails constructed on farms. The next class is the prisoner who has been given the option of a fine but who could not pay it. Farmers may inter-

view these men and try to persuade them to accept employment at current rates. The prisoner must remain in the
farmer's employment until he has completed the unexpired
portion of his sentence, or until he has earned enough to
pay the fine.

A second class is the prisoner with a sentence of three
months or less. He can be released on probation if he is willing to work out his sentence on a farm for not less than ten
cents a day.

A first offender with a sentence of from one to two years
may be given the opportunity of serving the second half of
his sentence on a farm at the going rate of pay.

Despite the efforts of the prison authorities, the convict-
labour system is abused, and the South African papers from
time to time report cases brought to court.

In July, 1959, an African boss-boy, J. Umvubu, was sentenced to three months for assaulting convict labourers. In
May, 1959, white farmer G. S. Lourens of Standerton district
appeared on the same charge. He was fined $140 or four
months, with a further two months imprisonment suspended.
In each of these cases it required a brave convict to press
charges, and there is no way of estimating how many suffered
in silence.

In June, 1959, Rachel Madeira applied for a writ of habeas
corpus for the return of her husband, Gabriel, a convict
labourer on the farm of one C. F. Grobler in the Trichardt
district. Mrs. Madeira swore that her husband had been re-
tained on the farm beyond the date when his sentence ex-
pired. The farmer had ruled that Madeira must stay on and
work out time lost when he was ill.

Madeira was found to be in hospital when the application
for the writ came before the Supreme Court in Pretoria. Ac-

cording to the Johannesburg *Star*, it was alleged that he was assaulted on the farm after he had visited a police station to request that he be discharged.

What of the ordinary farm labourer? It is virtually impossible for an African farm hand to become anything else, and the laws of Apartheid visit the same judgment on his children and their children. They must remain on the land.

The average wage in the Albany and Bathurst districts of the Eastern Cape for a farm worker and his family was in 1957 $25.20 a month. Payment was in cash and kind. In the Border Region forming the hinterland of East London a rural African earned $39.20 a year in cash and kind, engaging in subsistence agriculture in a native reserve. And returning to the heavily over-populated reserves is the only alternative Apartheid offers the farm labourer who works for a white farmer.

The exact extent of the reserves, where 3,651,830 Africans live, is not known because much of the land has not been surveyed. The government estimate is 16,929,224 morgen (a morgen is 2.1 acres) or 55,995 square miles, the equivalent of 11.9 per cent of the total area of the Union.

Apartheid on the land goes back to an act of 1913 that froze African land holdings. It prohibited them from purchasing or renting land outside the native reserves. However, recognizing that even then the reserves were overcrowded, provision was made for a commission to supervise increasing their size. Nothing happened until 1936, when it was decided that 7,500,000 morgen should be added to the reserves.

Since 1936 about three million of the promised 7,500,000 morgen have been added. Most of the new land has been poor and some had existing African population, and therefore did not ease overcrowding. It was suggested that at this rate of progress it would take another twenty-five years to buy the balance of the land required in 1936.

Supporters of Apartheid claim the reserves to be the best land in the country. In the Transkei some of the country is or has been good, and there is hope that in the future improved farming methods may restore this area. The problem is the result of over-grazing and of soil erosion. On top of this there are the results of usurious money lenders charging 100 per cent interest a month, illiteracy as high as 90 per cent, and only one doctor per twenty thousand population.

In the Northern Transvaal the reserves are situated mostly in dry bushveld country that affords little opportunity for agriculture or stock breeding. According to the Tomlinson report prepared by a government commission, "in general there are extremely low yields and declining productivity, gross overstocking and widespread soil erosion."

The report stated that 56 per cent of cattle deaths and 47 per cent of sheep deaths were caused by hunger and thirst. Average yield of maize on European farms was 6.98 bags per morgen, compared to 2.47 in the reserves.

"Farming in the Bantu areas," said the report, "is conducted on a sub-maintenance or poverty level. The result is that the vast majority of the families in the Bantu area are obliged to supplement their income from farming by selling their labour, not only outside agriculture but outside the Bantu areas as well. A genuine farming class practising progressive agriculture does not exist. As a consequence the Bantu pattern of farming is characterized by wrong use of the land, inefficient methods of cultivation, inefficient animal husbandry, increasing soil erosion, diminishing soil fertility, low yields from crops and livestock, extremely low incomes from farming, a qualitatively deficient diet, a low standard of health and a generally low standard of living."

These reserves or Bantu areas form what the architects of Apartheid call Bantustans. According to the theory, the simple African will live here in idyllic peace, happily reverting to the customs of their ancestors.

In 1936 the reserves were described in a White Paper as "congested, denuded, overstocked, eroded and for the most part in a deplorable condition". In 1948, the Assistant Director of Native Agriculture said of the Ciskei Reserve, "Over perhaps 10 per cent of the total area, the incidence of soil erosion may be described as slight; over 50 per cent as bad; over the balance as nothing less than terrifying."

The Native Laws Commission estimated that 30 per cent of the people living on the reserves already are landless. Twenty per cent of the arable land was termed unsuitable for cultivation.

Over half the children in the Transkei die before they are sixteen.

The South African Bureau of Race Relations (SABRA), the fountainhead of Apartheid doctrine, admitted that not 10 per cent of the Africans now living in Bantustans enjoy an "economic existence". The result is that the able-bodied men trek to the cities to obtain work. They are not permitted to take their families with them, and visitors to the reserves soon note the preponderance of children, women, and elderly people who are dependent on relatives working in the European areas.

One of the government solutions to the 1960 demonstrations was to arrest and pack off to the reservations hundreds of Africans in the cities who were classed as "loafers." The short-sightedness of this method was soon reflected in increasing political awareness among the rural population as the sophisticated city dwellers returned in exile.

Several astute observers suggested to me that it would be in the country districts rather than in the towns that the next racial explosion would occur. And it would be more likely to follow a Mau Mau pattern than the non-violent character of urban demonstrations.

Although it admits the poverty of the reserves and their inability to support the present population, SABRA clings to the vision of Bantustans accommodating "eventually in the native territories also all the descendants of those Bantu who have their homes on European farms and in the urban areas." In other words, three times the number of people who barely exist there today.

9. SCHOOL

NEWELL BANTU HIGH SCHOOL is in the African suburb of New Brighton, an appendage of the Indian Ocean city of Port Elizabeth. One day early in April, 1960, I had the privilege of giving a lesson on Canadian history and geography to Newell's graduating class. It was a moving experience as well as a revealing contact with Apartheid's grossest fraud, the Bantu Education Act, 1953.

Port Elizabeth is South Africa's largest wool-exporting centre and extremely sensitive to the effect that an international dock workers' blacklisting would have. One white business man assured me that it would bring down the Government within four days because of its impact on the back-country wool growers, who largely support the Nationalist party.

The town of Port Elizabeth was originally a military station at the end of the eighteenth century. When the British began to exploit their claim to the Cape after the Napoleonic Wars, 3,423 people, mostly English unemployed, were landed on Algoa Bay to form a settlement. Port Elizabeth's first impression on the world was as a source of ostrich feathers, and when this trade succumbed to new fashions, the town's prosperity was saved by wool and later by industrial development. North American automobile manufacturers chose it as the site for assembly plants.

The population of Port Elizabeth is 247,900, of whom 97,000 are white, 90,500 Africans, 5,300 Asian, and 54,200 mulatto. It and Pretoria are the only cities in the Union where the Europeans form the largest ethnic group.

New Brighton is the city's biggest African location. It is literally on the wrong side of the tracks and is reached by an Apartheid bridge over the railway yards. Appropriately, the bridge is divided into channels for Europeans and Africans. Although the Africans using the bridge outnumber the whites by more than a hundred to one, the European lane is twice as big as the African one.

As a slum, New Brighton goes back to the end of World War I. Barracks used by British troops of that era have been painted a dirty red and divided into housing for Africans. On a slightly higher level is Kwa Ford or Ford village, which owes its name to the contribution by the Ford Company of empty packing cases in which cars were shipped from Canada. The cases have been converted into two-room dwellings.

Rent for a two-room, semi-detached house is about $3.00 a month. There is no electricity, water is obtained from a communal tap, and plumbing is of the outdoor variety. A more recent development was the Economic Housing Scheme, a plan to encourage Africans to own their own homes by payment of $4.20 a month over a period of thirty years.

Africans are not allowed to own land, but there were sites in New Brighton where they could build their own homes. This was for the benefit of middle-class merchants and professional men with substantial incomes. There were only five doctors in the location, a ratio of one to 18,000 people (in Canada the ratio is regarded as satisfactory at one to 1,000). The doctors' usual fee was $3.50, including the provision of medicine; the average wage of their patients was about $1.50 a day.

There was one hospital in Port Elizabeth for non-Europeans and in New Brighton one prenatal clinic staffed with African nurses. Mothers lined up at the one baby clinic, where they paid fourteen cents a visit.

Barrack-like quarters for single men housed men from the reserves, who came in to work at the docks and on the railways. They, of course, were not allowed to bring their wives or families to the town with them.

Building had not kept pace with the needs of the African families whose right to live in the location met with approval. Some families waiting for homes still lived in disreputable shacks patched together from pieces of corrugated iron, flattened tins, scraps of plywood, and other industrial waste.

The land was poor, and only the middle-class residential section of the location had succeeded in making plants and hedges grow. The stucco cottages there were a cut above a North American slum.

Port Elizabeth was a stronghold of the African National Congress. In 1952 it had erupted into violent rioting; during the 1960 crisis it was ominously quiet, observing the National Day of Mourning for Sharpeville's dead but not answering the call of the Pan-Africanists, whose strength was on the Rand and at Cape Town.

Peter Mosenthal, president of the city's white chamber of commerce, said, "The time has arrived when organized commerce must make itself heard in the political arena. The Almighty has decided in his wisdom that South Africa was going to be a multi-racial country and the sooner people realize this the better."

Mr. Mosenthal's sensible words made no impression on the Government; they may have been a factor in maintaining the comparative calm in Port Elizabeth. But it was an uneasy lull. As I drove through New London there was none of the hostility to my white skin that I experienced in the African townships around Johannesburg. But going down the dusty roads and passing the idle groups of unemployed young men, I could see no good reason why one of them did not pick up one of the stones with which the ground was littered and fling it in my direction. If I had been in their place, I would have been sorely tempted to express my feeling with a well-aimed missile.

The little knots of idlers shooting dice straightened as my car hove in sight—it might have been a police patrol. There were a few youngsters hanging around each group, not asked into the game but ready to prove their usefulness by acting as watchdogs. There were little ones playing innocently in the dirt. These were the six out of every ten African children for whom there are no schools.

It is the boast of the Nationalist Government that before the Bantu Education Act came into force only 800,000 Africans could go to school. It is true that now there are 1,400,000 African pupils, and in the past fifteen years the number of schools for Africans has been doubled. This would be commendable progress had not the Bantu Education Act deliberately debased the standard of instruction provided. The quantity of schools may have been doubled, but the quality has been more than halved.

Newell Bantu High School came under the nefarious Act. It has 450 students, boys and girls, whose ambition was to obtain a university education. There would have been more pupils had there not been such a lack of accommodation. There was no problem of truancy in this school.

There was a wire fence around the grounds of the school and a good deal of effort had gone into growing grass at the front of the buildings. They were one-story structures, each housing two or three class-rooms. The principal's office was a small, crowded room near the main entrance. When I entered, unannounced, two African mothers were talking to the principal.

Logan K. Ntlabati, Newell's principal, was a tall, sturdily built man, obviously proud of his craft. The two mothers were pleading with him to find places for their children and he was refusing them as gently as he could. Every place in the school was occupied.

Mr. Ntlabati explained the sacrifice African parents made to send their children to school. Not only do they pay through their taxes $8,500,000 a year but they must buy text-books, and at Newell these cost as much as $40 in a year. This sum represents about the average wage for an African for one month.

The government subsidy for Bantu Education amounts to $18,200,000 a year, and the supporters of Apartheid pride themselves on their generosity. (They have a happy facility for overlooking the fact that the gold mines—some making profits of $2,800,000 a month—on which the country prospers, pay their employees about a nickel an hour and keep.) Not only is the subsidy less than two dollars per head of the African population, but at least some part of it is offered only on a cost-sharing system, and the school itself must put up dollar for dollar.

Newell's skimpy library was being built up sixpence by sixpence under the matching-grant scheme. To make up its share of the cost, the school put on exhibitions, concerts, and bazaars, charging nominal admission.

I asked about science and learned that there was a shortage of chemicals and laboratory equipment. In the entire school there was not one microscope, and I thought of the lavishly equipped North American high schools where such equipment is taken for granted. At Newell not only were there no microscopes, there were also no teaching aids to show students pictures of objects magnified many times. The science teacher did his best by drawing on the blackboard.

The first classroom I entered was the worst; the roof had buckled, the glass in some of the windows was broken, and the desks were ancient and dilapidated. A Canadian farmer would not have considered it fit for a chicken shed.

The graduating class I taught had better accommodation, although the desks were crowded together and the light was poor. The thirty-odd pupils rose at the entrance of their principal. He introduced me as a visitor from Canada and asked, "Who is the Prime Minister of Canada?"

A dozen brown arms shot up and a bright-faced boy gave the correct answer—"Diefenbaker." It was not a test I should have liked to try in my daughter's high school in Toronto. Her fellow students show little interest in current events, and it would not be likely that they could name the head of the South African Government.

With the aid of a tattered wall map of the North American continent I attempted to give them a little of my country's history and description. Thirty-odd pairs of brown eyes followed me intently; smiles broke out as I told them about the customs of the Eskimo, and a certain scepticism appeared when I explained what snow was like. Their appetite for knowledge was unlimited and I have never addressed such an attentive audience.

Chief Luthuli's parting words came back to me. When I had asked him what people outside South Africa could do, his first suggestion was the provision of scholarships that would enable young Africans to master the subjects they needed for self-government.

The Newell classes represented the brightest of these young people. Only 3.5 per cent of the pupils who get to school can be found places in secondary schools. The only career the Government encourages them to take is that of teaching, and only .7 per cent of South Africa's Negro students were in teacher-training colleges. And on the basis of government statements, it had been calculated that in the future there would be training facilities for only one African doctor per million of population.

Newell's students were eager for learning and they were being fobbed off with an inferior brand of curriculum and instruction. An educated African is a threat to white supremacy. He becomes what the racialists call "a cheeky Kaffir" and cannot be counted upon to accept his inferior status.

The Minister of Bantu Education makes no bones about his aims. "The paramount principle in the education of the child in the urban areas must be, just as it is in the reserves, that we must try to retain the child as a child of his own national community, because it is the basic principle of Bantu education in general that our aim is to keep the Bantu child a Bantu child. . . . The Bantu must be so educated that they do not want to become imitators [of the whites, but] that they will want to remain essentially Bantu."

Prime Minister Verwoerd has been more blunt. While he was Minister of Native Affairs he promised the Government would put an end within five or ten years to "that class of native who wants to become part of the European community." Under the United Party, he said, many schools had posed as the "great benefactors of the native peoples," and these schools—in many cases church schools—had taught the natives to become "black Englishmen".

The aim of the Bantu Education Act was explained by the Government Commission on Bantu Education. The African pupil was to learn just enough of the white languages—English and Afrikaans—to "follow oral or written instructions, and to carry on a simple conversation with Europeans about his work and other subjects of common interest." The African will receive an "education for natives as an independent race, in which their past and present, their inherent racial qualities, their distinctive characteristics and aptitudes and their needs under ever-changing social conditions are taken into consideration."

Dr. Albert Hertzog carried the racialists' arguments further. He said that most Africans obtain only four years of schooling, and that these should not be "wasted" by following European standards. The African should be taught only essentials he could not obtain elsewhere—hygiene, soil conservation, and cattle care.

Until the passing of the Bantu Education Act, church schools had provided most of the education for Africans. The Dutch Reformed Church, which provides the spiritual justification for Apartheid, was happy to transfer its mission schools to the State.

The Methodist Church flatly condemned the Act as "incompatible with Christian principles" and as "conditioning the African people to a predetermined position of subordination in the State." However, both the Methodist and Church of Scotland felt compelled to relinquish their schools to State control.

The Roman Catholics and the Seventh-Day Adventists decided to continue their own schools without government subsidy.

The Anglicans took the bitter step of closing their school. In Johannesburg Diocese, the Synod declared the new Act contrary to the will of God because it was based on Apartheid, because it attacked the natural rights and dignity of man, and because its aim was to ensure the perpetual domination by one racial group of another by intellectually starving it.

Prior to the Bantu Education Act, only about 5 per cent of the schools for Africans were government owned. The remainder were mission schools, where the Church provided the capital equipment but accepted a State subsidy to help meet operating expenses. As a result of the Act the situation is almost reversed, and the Government has protected itself against increases in cost by declaring a ceiling on subsidies for Bantu education, and declaring that any additional funds will have to come from the Africans themselves.

Another saving was effected by the Nationalist Government when it slashed the school meals scheme. According to the Orange Free State convention of the Nationalist Party, "European school feeding schemes tended to undermine the morale of the people and native school feeding constituted a financial burden that the Union's small white population could not continue to carry."

There was a Commission of Inquiry into School Feeding —South Africa has had so many commissions, studies, and reports that it is a statistician's paradise. The commission learned that there was wide-spread undernourishment, not only among the blacks but also among whites. The commission reported undernourishment of white children in 27.4 per cent of the areas investigated, of Africans in 65.3 per cent of the areas, of mulattoes in 44.8 per cent, and of Indians in 85.6 per cent. "The extent of undernourishment in the Union," said the report, "is of such a nature that comprehensive and active steps should be taken to raise the nutritional standard of the population."

Because they were over fourteen, the students in the graduating class at Newell Bantu High School were excluded from the Government's handsome school feeding subsidy of a little under a cent and a half a day. What of their future? They dearly wanted to go to a university if money and a place could be found.

Until Apartheid was imposed on education, the white University of Witwatersrand accepted about one hundred African students and the University of Cape Town about twice that number. At the University of Natal Africans were accepted but segregated. There is also an institution known as the University of South Africans open to Africans, but it conducts its classes by correspondence and is not strictly a university.

Apartheid descended on the universities under the misleading title of the Extension of University Education Act. The extension refers to the formation of colleges for non-whites. It is accompanied by a section barring entry of non-whites into existing universities.

The English-speaking universities unanimously condemned this imposed Apartheid. The Afrikaans-speaking universities officially subscribe to the government policy—they had never admitted non-whites—but there are rumbles of discontent from a handful of liberal Afrikaner intellectuals.

The new non-white colleges blatantly advertise their lack of any claim to university stature. The University College of the Western Cape was opened near Cape Town in March, 1960. Its premises are a former primary school. The Rector, J. G. Meiring, stated that its purpose was to prepare students for the professions. There is no medical school at this college and the only other profession people of mixed blood are permitted to enter is teaching.

The *Cape Argus,* a Cape Town newspaper, sent a correspondent to the new institution shortly after it was opened. He described being taken into the botany class by the Rector, who went up to one of the students and said: "Now look me straight in the eyes. I want you to answer this question, and I want you to tell me the truth. Don't tell me what you think I want to hear. And don't tell me a lie. Are you happy here?"

The *Cape Argus* solemnly reported that the student addressed gulped, smiled, and assured the Rector that he was perfectly happy.

The University College of Zululand is north of Durban, and while I was in that city the entire student body of the college walked out and went home. They claimed that the standard of instruction from the Afrikaner staff was so low that it was not worth their while to remain.

The two other African "universities" are the University College of the North in the Transvaal for the Sotho people, and Fort Hare, near Grahamstown, for the Xhosas.

Fort Hare was once respected for its high standards. Opened in 1916 by General Botha, it catered mainly but not exclusively to Africans. Among the Africans were only 38 per cent Xhosa; 34 per cent came from other African communities; 14 per cent were Coloured, and 14 per cent Indian.

The Minister of Bantu Education told Parliament that Fort Hare was nothing but an English university for non-whites. English had to be used as a language because the students came from so many different backgrounds. As a result the Xhosa students were neglecting their own languages and traditions. If they talked Xhosa instead, that language would eventually reach the status of a university language.

In the past, the Minister continued, white and non-white persons had served on the Council and the Senate and had been accommodated on a basis of equality. This custom must inevitably create a fallacious impression among the non-whites that Apartheid was something that disappeared when one reached a certain academic level. It might even suggest that academic training would remove discrimination in South Africa. The result would be that students would become agitators against the racial order in South Africa.

The Minister took over Fort Hare, got rid of the governing body with its mixture of white and black, and fired the principal; the heads of the departments of law, English, philosophy, politics, and geography; the registrar, a lecturer, and the librarian. Fort Hare was degraded to a tribal college.

Enrolment of new students dropped from 120 in 1959 to sixty-nine in 1960. The student body courageously stated: "The Government, in its dictatorial action in dismissing our staff members without stating any reasons, has added to the atmosphere of insecurity and uncertainty that has engulfed Fort Hare during the past few years. The atmosphere makes the normal pursuit of academic activities almost impossible.

"But let it be noted, once and for all, that our stand as students of Fort Hare and as the future leaders of our country, upholding the principles of education as universally accepted, remains unchanged and uncompromising. Our outright condemnation of university Apartheid legislation remains steadfast.

"We wish to warn the architects of white domination, the whole country and the world at large that we will not be held responsible for the disastrous repercussions of this Apartheid policy, which in the foreseeable future will destroy the entire social, political and economic structure of our country."

10. CHURCHES

FATHER CYPRIAN THORPE was sitting in his cellar study, wrestling with paper work, when I called on him in Port Elizabeth. His coat was off but he still had on the clerical bib that contrasted with the brawny arms exposed by rolled-up sleeves. In appearance he was still a beefy English parson, although he had been toiling in South Africa for the past twenty-four years.

Holy Spirit Mission in New Brighton was his charge. The Church of England subsidized him with missionary funds, but the bulk of his finance, including a $65,000 church a-building, came from his African parishioners. Two churches in the Walmer location had been burned down during the restive period since the Sharpeville massacre. But it was not burning of churches that worried Father Thorpe. He was concerned about the families of men and women detained under the Emergency Regulations.

Thirty-seven people had been seized on March 30, when the Special Branch of the South African police enjoyed its first taste of power under the police-state provisions of the Public Safety Act. At least, thirty-seven was the total reached by Father Thorpe after arduous investigation. The police were not telling anyone whom or how many they had pulled in without warrant; and the law made it illegal for anyone to tell even an Anglican missionary that a man was in jail and his children left to starve.

Almost all the police victims were Africans. The only two whites to be arrested were a man regarded by liberals as a police *provocateur* who joined political groups in order to inform on them, and a do-gooder whose only known offence was that he organized emergency feeding schemes to relieve African hunger.

Father Thorpe's worn notebook showed a terrible similarity about the arrested Africans. Nearly all of them were young men with young families—a bus conductor with five children, the eldest ten; an office boy with four youngsters; a labourer with a pregnant wife; and, the most desperate case, a widower with three orphaned children. In the one case where both husband and wife were arrested, fortunately there were no children.

The day after the arrests had been made, Father Thorpe went to the magistrate to ask permission to see the detainees. All South Africa was floundering inside the new restrictions and officialdom was taking no chances. The magistrate sent him to the chief of police of the uniformed branch, who in turn suggested the chief jailer. At the jail, the priest found a dozen African women who had brought food and clothes to their husbands. They were being chased away by white warders.

The jail governor was no help. He was under orders from the Special Branch of the police, and his interpretation of his instructions was that these wicked detainees were not even to be seen by the regular prison chaplain.

The detainees' wives unloaded their problems onto Father Thorpe's ample shoulders. They were minor matters, but enough to create a crisis in an African household. One man had been snatched away without time to leave the key for the family cash box. Another had been bundled into jail complete with the rent book, and without that document his family was quite likely to be evicted from their home.

The priest managed to intercede with the authorities and straighten out these crises. That left him with the original problem: who was going to feed the families? The magistrate advised Father Thorpe that under law such and such of Apartheid, he would have to establish and register a special fund with the authorities before he could solicit any money. The permission would likely be granted after an application had been duly considered.

Somehow, in the first week after the arrests $135 found its way into Father Thorpe's pockets without a suspicion of solicitation. (It was significant that more than half the funds raised for the legal defence and physical welfare of the treason-trial victims and their families—some $175,000—was contributed within South Africa.)

Father Thorpe hoped to find a Roman Catholic family that would "adopt" the widower's youngest daughter. She was at a church boarding school and $81 would pay her fees for the year. But nearly $3,000 a month would be needed to keep the other thirty-six fatherless families above the subsistence level.

Now when I hear of a new wave of South African arrests or read the impressive total of detainees announced from time to time in Parliament, I think both of the individuals who have been seized and of their families, who also suffer. And I remember Father Thorpe bravely trying to ease their misery.

Father Thorpe was one of those Anglican missionaries whose efforts on behalf of the Africans were recognized by the Government with the arrest of two of them under the

Emergency Regulations: Father Mark Nye, head of the Pretoria Anglican Mission, and Miss Hannah Stanton, Warden of the Tumelong Anglican Mission, Pretoria.

The attitude of these people was probably best summed up by Father Trevor Huddleston in his book, *Naught for Your Comfort:* *

> I believe that because God became Man, therefore human nature in itself has a dignity and a value which is infinite. I believe that this conception necessarily carries with it the idea that the State exists for the individual, not the individual for the State. Any doctrine based on racial or colour prejudice and enforced by the State is therefore an affront to human dignity and, *ipso facto,* an insult to God himself. It is for this reason that I feel bound to oppose not only the policy of the present Government of the Union of South Africa but the legislation that flows from this policy.

I first met Father Huddleston at Mirfield, Yorkshire, where the Community of the Resurrection has its conventual church. Huddleston had recently been recalled there by the order, from his post in Johannesburg. A tall man wearing a white monkish habit, he had an ascetic face; yet he combined his priestly appearance with a down-to-earth outlook.

With him that day was a young American from Groton College, who had decided to study for the priesthood and had come to Huddleston for guidance. He was a brilliant student, a star athlete, and a musician. "Just the type we need," Huddleston told me, "and besides he blows a very hot trumpet."

The Father Huddleston Jazz Band was still going strong

* New York: Doubleday & Company, Inc., 1956. London: Wm. Collins Sons & Co., Ltd., 1956.

in Johannesburg, and its patron explained to me his theory that the best way to get to white South Africans was through the media of jazz and sport. Thanks to his efforts, the British Musicians' Union has barred any of its members from appearing in South Africa until the Apartheid system has ended.

The meaning of Father Huddleston's remarks about sport were brought home to me when I was in South Africa. After the Emergency Regulations had been imposed, the newspapers were treading warily in their reporting of police brutality, but they gave banner headlines to rugger and cricket tours that had become entangled in politics as a result of South Africa's rigid Apartheid in organized sport. The New Zealand rugger team, the All-Blacks, kept South Africa on tenterhooks for several weeks before deciding to visit that country. The Welsh trade unions had threatened to boycott any South African rugger team that visited their land, and Rev. Dick Sheppard, one of Britain's finest cricketers, had refused to play against the South African team. In each of these cases I could discern the fine hand of Trevor Huddleston.

Hannah Stanton was a tall, attractive Englishwoman of forty-four. For three years she was warden of the Tumelong Mission in the Lady Selborne African location outside Pretoria. There she ran a nursery school where three hundred children were cared for, and a training school for African social workers. This was the only school of its kind in the country. Its students were being taught how to work in locations, providing badly needed social services—helping families solve financial problems and difficulties arising from the pass laws, and assisting people whose relatives were in trouble with the police.

Her crime in the eyes of the South African police was that she treated Africans as human beings. Her home was one of the few places where white and black were treated equally. She was also suspected of counselling victims of police brutality to file legal action claiming damages.

On Thursday, March 24, 1960, at their usual hour of 3 A.M., a party of Special Branch police and a prison wardress barged into Tumelong Mission, where Miss Stanton and three other European missionaries lived. They flourished a warrant and began searching the premises. The wardress accompanied Miss Stanton while she dressed and even insisted on accompanying her to the bathroom.

The five plain-clothes men pounced on a copy of the Liberal Party newspaper *Contact,* a leaflet about the Accra Conference, and a treason-trial bulletin, all of which could be purchased openly in South Africa. They also seized two personal notebooks, and scrupulously wrote out receipts for all the material they took away.

"This," said Miss Stanton, "is an experience that not infrequently befalls our African neighbours. It is a new one for us."

Exactly six days later, the police returned at the same hour. This time they were without a warrant. (In a bit of bungling that will be explained later, they had jumped the gun on the imposition of Emergency Regulations.) Miss Stanton was hauled off to Central Prison, Pretoria.

It was a mark of the inefficiency as much as of the vindictiveness of the South African police state that Hannah Stanton was kept in solitary confinement. She was the only white woman imprisoned under the Emergency Regulations in

Pretoria. Her jailers were ordered to keep her apart from ordinary prisoners, and because she was only one of her kind she was held incommunicado.

Five weeks after her arrest, the Government got around to passing a law under which Hannah Stanton could be deported.

What the police had hoped to find when they raided Tumelong Mission were some of the depositions made by the wounded victims of the Sharpeville massacre. An independent investigation of Sharpeville had been undertaken by Miss Stanton's fellow Anglican, Dr. Ambrose Reeves, the Bishop of Johannesburg.

A doughty fighter against Apartheid, Bishop Reeves had formed a committee immediately after the police shootings. Two lawyers, John Lang and Ernest Wentzel, were commissioned to gather evidence; and before the police realized what was happening, they managed to interview and take statements from some of the wounded. These documents were the first indication of what was later confirmed at the official inquiry by Dr. John Friedman, who performed the autopsies, and Dr. P. Keen, who examined the wounded—that 70 per cent of the Sharpeville victims were shot in the back.

Land and Wentzel were among the first to be arrested under the Emergency Regulations on March 30. Bishop Reeves was busy that day securing legal aid for them and other detainees in Johannesburg. When I reached him by telephone at noon, his immediate reaction to my Canadian accent was, "How good to hear a voice from the outside world!" He explained that he was waiting to hear from his own lawyers whether the Emergency Regulations permitted him to make a statement, but that he would be pleased to see me that afternoon.

"Did you see Ambrose Reeves?" was the first question put to me by the Special Branch during my farcical interrogation in Durban jail. No courtesy in the way of using his title of bishop. The way it was said, it sounded like "the criminal Ambrose Reeves". And I imagine that both his dossier and mine now record that we have met.

Bishop Reeves was a small man. Bright blue eyes danced behind the spectacles on his deeply lined, tanned face. He was no stranger to race problems, having served in the multi-racial diocese of Liverpool and spent some time in the southern United States. He explained to me that his lawyers had advised him that to issue any statement would be to court his own arrest, but that he would be glad to speak to me off the record.

We talked about the Sharpeville massacre, and he said what was later to be published as an appeal for aid to the victims: "I would go into a court of law and say, if it were the last thing I ever did, that it was not necessary for the police to open fire. One woman was in a shop buying groceries. Another was hanging out washing in a back yard. Even if there were provocation, it is difficult to believe that it could have been sufficiently serious to warrant what can only be described as a massacre of unarmed people."

The bishop described the crisis as the result of a series of lost opportunities. "Ten years ago," he said, "we could still think in terms of doing good *for* the African. Now we must work *with* him or he'll throw anything we do back in our face. And the time when we can work *with* the Africans is fast running out.

"We must persuade these people in the Government to sit

around and talk with the African leaders. Their most fantastic mistake has been to arrest the African leaders and ban their organizations. The whole crux of the problem is consultation. You can't rule the country by force."

Bishop Reeves approved my idea of moving on to Cape Town, but when I asked him if he could suggest anyone to see there, he gave me one name and stopped to think. "All the others," he said at last, "are in jail."

The bishop himself was in peril of imprisonment, and there must have been some interesting debate between senior police officers and itchy fingers as they considered whom they would arrest.

The following Sunday I heard the South African Broadcasting Corporation issue a news bulletin that Bishop Reeves was "taking a brief holiday in the country". This was more than a social note, and the message between the lines was that the outspoken bishop had not been arrested. Rumours of his arrest and that of Archbishop Hurley, the Roman Catholic prelate in Durban, were frequently heard and much time had to be spent in proving them false.

Dr. Reeves was in fact on his way out of South Africa. Two days after his two lawyers had been jailed, he had received a visit at 9:30 P.M. from some friends who informed him that he was to be jailed under the Emergency Regulations. The bishop consulted his clerical advisers and decided he could do more good fighting Apartheid from abroad.

Such decisions are difficult to make. Should one seek martyrdom, or should one choose to carry on the struggle in exile? It was harrowing even to watch, as I did in Cape Town, an honest man trying to make that choice. It was in the office of Patrick Duncan, a son of a former South African Governor-General. The telephone rang while a few correspondents were talking to him in his office as editor of the Liberal weekly *Contact*.

Duncan took the call calmly and there was no indication from his part of the conversation of its threatening nature. When he put down the receiver, he turned and asked us to excuse him, but he had just received word that he was about to be arrested.

Leaning back in his chair, Duncan opened an argument with one of his assistants as to the duty of a liberal. Should he submit to arbitrary arrest, or should he go underground? Should he try to remain inside the country, or should he present the case against Apartheid in other countries?

There was such an unreal atmosphere about the discussion that one of us asked Duncan whether he had made any preparations. Were his affairs in order and, most important, did he have any clean underwear? Another assistant editor dashed out of the office and returned with an assortment of clean clothes that he had kept for such an emergency. Duncan deliberately straightened the papers on his desk, carefully put the cover on his typewriter, and asked apologetically if we would mind if he went for a short walk.

Duncan chose to disappear. The first warning proved to be a false alarm, but he later received other tips of police intentions and he suspended the publication of his paper.

Bishop Reeves' departure did not leave the Anglicans leaderless. In Cape Town Archbishop Joost de Blank continued the Christian opposition to Apartheid. His appointment was almost a stroke of luck for the Church of England. A Dutchman, educated in a British public school and university, his career has a slight resemblance to that of Dr. Verwoerd, also Dutch born and an immigrant to South Africa.

"I am a man in high office who was born in another country," he once told some of his critics. "I should be happy to leave South Africa if I could be accompanied by that other person in high office who was born in the same country."

For the first year of his archbishopric, Dr. de Blank imposed silence on himself as far as Apartheid was concerned. The attitude of the Anglican church, he said, was well known, but, as a new boy, he first wanted to learn the ropes before speaking out.

Archbishop de Blank's strategy was to apply pressure on the Dutch Reformed Church in the hope that it might withdraw the scriptural sanction it had given to Apartheid. The Dutch Reformed Churches—there are three of them—command the respect of the Afrikaners; and if they could be persuaded to shift their attitude on segregation it would have considerable impact on the Government. To achieve this aim, Dr. de Blank decided to work through the World Council of Churches, and to this body he sent his archdeacon as an envoy.

Archdeacon Cecil Wood called on Dr. Willem Visser 't Hooft, the general secretary of the World Council, with the Archbishop's request for a fact-finding team to visit South Africa and study the racial situation. The council dispatched its associate secretary-general on a reconnaissance. On his return, Dr. Robert Bilheimer declared that the state of affairs was so complex it appeared to be "inextricable."

Nor did the move endear the Archbishop to the Afrikaners. *Die Burger,* the Cape Town Nationalist newspaper, declared that "after years of sporadic sparring, Archbishop Joost de Blank has now started a total war on the Dutch Reformed Church, for this is what his new action against the Church amounts to."

The moderator of the Dutch Reformed Synod of Cape

Province accused Dr. de Blank of pointing "an unclean finger of accusation". The statement went on to say, "We cannot condone the continued besmirching of our country with false information."

This charge came strangely from the Church that supports the Government whose segregation laws include a clause under which authorities can limit church services to members of any designated race. "Under the limiting regulations," Archbishop de Blank pointed out, "anyone from another race group attending a service lays himself open to grave penalties, including flogging."

Replying to the Dutch Reformed Church's attack, Dr. de Blank said the crucial issue is whether racial discrimination in church and state has been repudiated. "I know," he said, "the Anglicans have failed again and again in putting fundamental Christian principles into practice. We have no illusions and are deeply penitent for our failures.

"But as a church we have repudiated Apartheid at the highest level and are seeking to eradicate it in all our churches and institutions."

The Dutch Reformed Church preaches a fundamentalist religion derived from Calvinism. It has three branches.

The Nederduits Gereformeerde Kerk (NGK), with more than a million members, is the largest branch. Its ministers included the former Prime Minister, the late Dr. Daniel F. Malan.

The Nederduits Hervormde Kerk (NHK), with about 130,000 members, is strongest in the Transvaal, where it was formed to care for the Trekkers who had lost touch with the parent church at the Cape. Its members are called Doppers.

The Gereformeerde Kerk, with less than 100,000 members, is the smallest of the three, but it exerts a power out of proportion to its size. This is partly because of the narrowness and rigidness of its Calvinism, and partly because so many of its members go in for the ministry and for teaching. It also claims to be the original offshoot of the mother church in Holland and to have been founded by Van Riebeeck, the founder of the original Cape settlement.

The three share the Calvinistic doctrine of predestination, from which is developed the theory that the Afrikaners are a chosen people, selected by God to rule in South Africa. This is coupled with a belief in the inborn inferiority of the African and the notion that his ignorance and disease are the product of an ordained defect.

Significantly, there is a trend against colour discrimination. At the height of the 1960 crisis, twelve influential dominies of the Dutch Reformed Church condemned the Government's Apartheid policy. They did not lend their names to this statement of revolt, but they promised to bring together a hundred ministers who shared their views. They stated their:

—rejection of enforced Apartheid as unethical and without any foundation in Scripture;

—alarm at the way in which Apartheid is causing hatred, increasing racial tension and widening the gulf between the races;

—agreement, as individuals, to speak out in the interests of right and justice.

The twelve took the unusual course of presenting their change in belief to an Afrikaner Member of Parliament, Japie Basson. An able and attractive politician in his early forties, Basson broke away from the Nationalists to form his own one-man National Union. He was gaining political strength, commanding large audiences at public meetings, when the

Sharpeville massacre took place and the Government retaliated by banning meetings.

The twelve dominies told Basson that they considered Apartheid the most important political question in South Africa. Government measures causing extreme misery and hatred were cited as:

—race classification, in which families were broken up on the grounds of colour;

—job reservation, in which people were deprived of the right to earn a living at the calling they might have followed for years;

—the Mixed Marriages Act;

—harsh implementation of the pass laws;

—constant liquor raids on African locations;

—restrictions on holding church services for Africans in white areas;

—the policy preventing African servants in towns from living together with their husbands on their employers' property.

The twelve dominies were not calling for integration, but in contemporary South Africa their discussion with Basson was almost heretical. The reforms they suggested were not a wholesale rejection of Apartheid, but rather a softening of its harshness.

Yet the stand of these twelve was one of the most hopeful signs in the South Africa of 1960.

11. VERWOERD

ONE OF THE Nationalist Government's reactions to the Sharpeville massacre was to ban all public meetings in the Transvaal and Natal for a period of three months. This effectively squelched Japie Basson's growing National Union movement for the time being; it had no effect whatsoever on Prime Minister Hendrik Frensch Verwoerd. He had scheduled a *stryddag* or rally at the village of Meyerton for Saturday, March 26; and a *stryddag* there would be, even if the Africans were mourning their dead not a dozen miles away and no other group was permitted to meet in public.

It could be said of Dr. Verwoerd that he is a devout Calvinist and the father of seven children. Further than that, on the credit side, I find it difficult to go. If he must be granted sincerity in his patriotism, then it is the sincerity of a Hitler or a Stalin. If he appears to have intellectual stature, it is only in comparison with the moss-backs and small-minded bigots surrounding him.

Dr. Verwoerd repeatedly calls himself a Christian, yet he is the most ruthless exponent of the unchristian doctrines of Apartheid and *baasskap*. He claims South Africa is in the forefront of Western civilization; but he is turning it into a police state. He dedicates himself to fight Communism, and creates the conditions under which it can flourish. He deludes his own partisans, telling them he will save them from being swallowed up by the Africans, while, in fact, he speeds the day of the holocaust.

The Prime Minister was born in Holland and brought to South Africa at the age of one. He was schooled in Afrikaner institutions and went to Germany for post-graduate work in his chosen field of psychology. He became Professor of Applied Psychology at the Afrikaner University of Stellenbosch.

His first recorded public pronouncement was a call in 1936 to bar South Africa's doors to the Jewish refugees from Hitler's Germany. The next step was to become editor of the Nationalist paper *Die Transvaaler,* a post he held from 1939 until 1948. During the war years *Die Transvaaler* was undisguisedly anti-British, and its pro-Nazism was thinly veiled. When another South African paper commented on his pro-German bias, Dr. Verwoerd sued for damages—and lost. The judge ruled that he had knowingly given support to the enemy.

When the late King George VI took the Royal Family to South Africa in 1947, not one word of their presence was allowed to appear in *Die Transvaaler.* When the royal party arrived in Johannesburg for one of the biggest festivals the city had ever seen, Dr. Verwoerd unbent to the extent of reporting for his readers that traffic might be congested that day. There was no explanation why.

With the backing of the Broederbond, the immensely powerful Afrikaner secret society, Dr. Verwoerd became a Senator in 1948 and was appointed to the Cabinet portfolio of Native Affairs. It was the year that the Nationalists under Dr. Daniel Malan for the first time came to full power on a program of Apartheid.

Dr. Verwoerd was the architect in charge of erecting the structure of *baasskap* society. No one was more passionately dedicated to his work. He began unfolding a blueprint for the salvation of "Western Christian civilization" and the permanent relegation of the African to sub-human status. He became the chief hot gospeller of Apartheid.

Malan retired and was replaced by Johannes Gerhardus Strijdom, the "Lion" (or Messiah) of the North. The campaign to continue separating European and non-European in every walk of life continued. So drastic were some of the Strijdom-Verwoerd measures that some Nationalists began to worry about the doctrinaire rigidity of their leaders. Dr. Malan had repudiated the goal of total Apartheid; Strijdom and Verwoerd reinstituted it, conceding that while immediate complete Apartheid was impractical, a start should be made "on a long path".

Strijdom's death was followed in 1958 by a Nationalist Party caucus to choose a new leader. The principal candidates were Theophilus Ebenhaezer Dönges and Hendrik Frensch Verwoerd. Dönges had succeeded Dr. Malan as Nationalist leader in the Cape. His approach to racial problems was that Apartheid was the least of three evils—a mixed society, abandoning South Africa, or keeping the Africans segregated. Verwoerd took a positive line; he alone had the solution—*baasskap* and an Afrikaner republic, with a president "responsible only to God".

Verwoerd dominated the caucus and became Prime Minister.

Prime Minister Verwoerd signalled full steam ahead towards Apartheid. During his first year in office he unveiled the Bantu Self-Government Bill and told Parliament it would have thirty-seven hours to debate it before he called in his majority phalanx to make the bill law. It was a measure that set back South Africa three hundred years by abolishing all African representation in Parliament.

In place of the seven elected representatives, whites who spoke for the African, there would be eight African "national" units with Commissioners-General to report back to the white man's Parliament. The national units would have "self-government" of all their "important affairs". These turned out to be regulating markets, licensing building, administering trading sites, and taxation. Even these were subject to the will of the white Parliament.

The first so-called "African self-government" was instituted in the Transkei on the reservations belonging to the mythical Apartheid state of Bantustan. This is the home of about 1,500,000 Africans supposedly enjoying "separate development".

According to Robert Nielsen, Associate Editor of *The Toronto Star*'s editorial page, who replaced me in South Africa after my expulsion, "politically, the embryo of self-government is barely pulsing in the Transkei. The black Parliament meeting here is obviously (and perhaps necessarily) run by white advisers. The Government took care to eliminate in advance any chance of a live opposition, by deposing or exiling unruly chiefs."

Nielsen went to Umtata, near East London, to attend the sitting of the Bunga, where 123 chiefs and headmen met for the annual session of the Transkeian Territorial Authority. This is the body that Dr. Verwoerd trumpets as progress for the African, yet its sessions were run by its white secretary, C. B. Young.

"Young dominated the opening session," Nielsen reported, "and left no doubt where the real power lay. He said native objectives in South Africa cannot be achieved by violence, intimidation and crime but only through bodies created by the white Parliament. He heaped scorn on agitators who, he said, were trying to usurp the authority of the chiefs. These agitators could not bring higher wages, better housing, education and industrial development to the natives.

" 'Only you chiefs in co-operation with the Government can do that,' Young said."

Despite their marching orders, two members of the Bunga bravely criticized Dr. Verwoerd's policy of moving "surplus" Africans from the white areas to the reserves. And they frankly stated the starvation conditions and the number of landless people amongst the nearly four million now on the reserves.

The Bunga was also instructed by its white secretary to work out a method of reimposing the chief's tribal authority over the 2,600,000 Africans who now live in South African cities. Some of them have been there for two and three generations, yet their only means of political representation is to be through "ambassadors" from the chiefs in Bantustan.

This was how the dream world of Dr. Verwoerd was functioning in March, 1960. The urban Africans, oppressed by low wages, high rents, and food costs, rebelled against that aspect of Apartheid that humiliated them most—the pass laws. They demonstrated at Langa and Nyanga, outside Cape Town and at Sharpeville.

Police guns were no sooner silent than Dr. Verwoerd was on his feet in Parliament. "The riots," he declared, "can in no way be described as reactions against the Government's Apartheid policy. The disturbances are a periodic phenomenon and have got nothing to do with poverty and low wages."

This incredible statement is a frank expression of Nationalist Government policy. And Dr. Verwoerd was to repeat it for those who, at first, failed to grasp its significance. Where three million whites intend to hold ten million blacks in semi-slavery, riots and strong-arm suppression must be accepted as the South African way of life. The Government did not promise there would be no repetition of the Sharpeville massacre. On the contrary, Dr. Verwoerd made plain there would be repeated African demonstrations. His only promise was that the Government would put down these protests firmly and promptly.

It would be seen, Dr. Verwoerd told Parliament, that the rioting did not really have anything to do with South African policy. It had nothing to do with the reference books against which the campaign was aimed. There had been similar trouble in the Belgian Congo, the Cameroons, Nyasaland, and other countries. South Africa had been lucky, for it had been spared disturbances as big as those in other countries.

Dr. Verwoerd said his first duty was to thank the South African police on behalf of the House and the people for the courageous, efficient way they handled the situation. The police at times found it difficult to control themselves, but they had done so in an exemplary manner.

It might be argued that the Prime Minister was misinformed, and it may be significant that the national chief of police, Major-General C. I. Rademeyer, was reported to have been replaced on account of what was described as a "sudden illness" after the shooting had died down. How else than by being led astray by his subordinates could the Prime Minister term the police work "courageous" and "efficient," when at Sharpeville 70 per cent of its victims were shot in the back?

Police surgeons knew these people were shot in the back, the Bishop of Johannesburg knew it, and the world was told officially on May 3 by Dr. John Friedman, senior district surgeon of Johannesburg, testifying at the judicial inquiry into Sharpeville. It is conceivable that the information was concealed from Dr. Verwoerd. In the past, he had been known to insulate himself from unpleasant facts and, on one occasion, when invited to inspect Johannesburg's African slums, admitted that his knowledge was based on an airplane flight over them.

In his own little dream world, Dr. Verwoerd concocted for Parliament his explanation of the Sharpeville and Langa demonstrations. He believed the agitation behind the riots was on a nation-wide scale. The present wave of excitement among Africans drew much of its force and direction from sustained attacks that had been made on the Government's policy over the past ten years. The arguments used by those determined to get the Nationalist Party out of power—especially newspaper reports, which concentrated on sensationalism above all else—had brought about a spirit of resistance among Africans.

I was to hear this smug theory again after my own imprisonment and the unfortunate assassination attempt on Dr. Verwoerd. It was parroted by the arrogant Minister for External Affairs, Eric Hendrik Louw, who tried to prove that the misguided man who had shot at the Prime Minister had been inspired by reading "sensational newspaper reports".

Immediately on my arrival in South Africa I telegraphed the Government's Chief Information Officer, Piet Meiring, in Cape Town requesting an interview with the Prime Minister at his convenience. After several days a reply came saying that Dr. Verwoerd was too busy. The next best thing was to watch him in action, and I travelled to Meyerton, about thirty-five miles from Johannesburg, to attend the March 26 *stryddag*.

Meyerton is a Transvaal village on the veld that is similar to any North American prairie town—a few shops clustered near the cross-roads, a post office, a small hotel, and the Dutch Reformed Church. On the outskirts were a football field and a fairground.

It was 2:30 on the afternoon of an early South African autumn day when I arrived at Meyerton. Although the Prime Minister was not to speak until six, preparations were well under way, and a crowd of sturdy farm folk from the surrounding area was beginning to gather. Booths had been erected and the good Boer housewives had loaded plank counters with samples of their home cooking and baking. In one corner of the ground a lone African was stoking the barbecue coals for the roasting of the local farm sausage. With the exception of a browbeaten elderly man busy picking up scraps of paper, he was the only African I was to see all day.

Other cooks mixed batter for the sweet pancakes that were to stave off our hunger during the next seven hours. There was the ubiquitous Coca-Cola stand, seeming out of place in this chauvinistic setting; and later an empty Coca-Cola case was placed on the platform to allow child speakers to reach the microphone.

Dr. Verwoerd's picture hung from poles. "Ons Man" the inscription began—"Our Man Can Hold His Own." In other posters he was joined by his predecessors, Gen. Hertzog, Dr. Malan, and Strijdom, demonstrating his allegiance to the true Afrikaner faith.

Another banner proclaimed Dr. Verwoerd "the greatest statesman of the West", a claim that would not be challenged in Meyerton but which struck me with the recollection that since General Smuts was defeated in 1948, South Africa had made no contribution whatsoever to the international scene.

Girl Guides (Afrikaner segregated type—the international Boy Scout and Girl Guide movement believes in mixed units) moved through the crowd selling pins celebrating the Union's fiftieth anniversary.

Overhead a couple of Harvard training planes of the South African Air Force lazily patrolled the cloudless sky. They were controlled by a ground crew in a radio-equipped jeep. Police cruisers whipped up and down the roads leading in and out of town, and my South African colleagues at the press table pointed out the more obvious plain-clothes men from the police Special Branch who mingled in the crowd.

Three bearded patriarchs wearing broad-brimmed bush hats were installed on the platform. They were tall, stern-faced men who would have been more at home in the era of President Oom Paul Kruger, who sat on his verandah at Pretoria and if any of his people had a complaint, invited them to "come and drink coffee with me". Nowadays one of Dr. Verwoerd's secretaries sees that complaints are transmitted through proper party channels, and there is little communication between the Prime Minister and the country folk who keep him in power.

Sitting at the press table at the foot of the rough platform, my colleague Gerald Clark of the *Montreal Star* and I were easily recognizable as overseas visitors. A choleric gentleman who introduced himself as a government purchasing agent took the opportunity to belabour us for misreporting the South African scene. Ninety-nine per cent of what was written about the country was false, he maintained. When we tried to pin him down to specific examples, it turned out that he was particularly cross with John Gunther and Adlai Stevenson, both of whom had had the temerity to make statements about the Union of South Africa without having had the grace to live their lives there.

His anti-Americanism had been rekindled by the U.S. government statement after Sharpeville: "The United States deplores violence in all its forms and hopes the African people of South Africa will be able to obtain redress for their grievances by peaceful means. While the United States as a matter of practice does not ordinarily comment on the internal affairs of governments with which it enjoys normal relations, it cannot help but regret the tragic loss of life resulting from the measures taken against the demonstrators in South Africa."

"The next step," this hysterical extremist yelled at us, "will be the Yanks sending an army to invade South Africa. Don't think they won't." We tried to reassure him on this score but he wouldn't have it. In his role as purchasing agent he had instituted a boycott of all U.S. products.

After telling us to look at the million-dollar hospitals "we built for the dirty Kaffirs," his parting remark was "if we go down, we'll pull the English with us." This was the rabid Nationalist, unabashedly declaring his scorn for the African and his belief in violent means of "keeping the Kaffir in his place". Later, it was Dr. Verwoerd's function to provide the respectable gloss for these theories.

It was 6:30 before the Prime Minister's cavalcade arrived and he was escorted to the platform under a crude poster showing him holding back the black tide sweeping south over Africa. The crowd filled the field—about fifteen thousand men, women, and children, and by no means the palpable exaggeration of sixty to eighty thousand claimed by the Nationalist press.

The meeting began in a revivalist atmosphere created by

Afrikaner songs sounding like camp-fire hymns. A dominie read from the Scripture and offered a long prayer. And then a troop of youngsters were led to the platform to struggle with memorized tributes to the Prime Minister, the Nationalist Party, and South Africa.

"We ask the world," pleaded one sausage-curled youngster, "not to condemn us for we are trying to preserve a precious heritage."

It was 7:26 when Dr. Verwoerd rose to speak. He was a tall figure, with a thin smile on his fresh, avuncular countenance. His words came slowly but distinctly; it was the performance of a professor and not a rabble rouser.

He began in Afrikaans, but on four occasions during his hour-and-a-half address he broke into English. With an almost 100 per cent Afrikaner audience, his English remarks obviously were directed at the press table.

"The mass of blacks are law-abiding," he began, "but there are agitators among them. We must not misunderstand the Bantu in our midst. I have much experience of the Bantu throughout South Africa and they are loyal to the Government and Administration of the country.

"We don't intend to be perturbed about what is done and said in the outside world in all ignorance. Those who see from afar do not always see correctly. We intend to do what is just and right as a Christian nation in dealing with the people and fellow-men in this country of ours. We realize there is a common basis of humanity."

He spoke of Apartheid, "the policy in which we believe and which is as much in their interest as our own." The voice grew unctuous as he declared, "We are not the oppressors we are made out to be. We are Christians. We have a conscience as others have.

"We also realize—which the outside world often does not—that you do not only have to take into consideration the rights of the black man, but that there is also a white man. The white man brought civilization to this country, and all that you see which the Bantu has inherited today was created by the knowledge and diligence of the white man."

There was no heckling. The crowd was with Dr. Verwoerd but it was not swayed by him. If there were no interruptions, neither were there any bursts of cheering.

"In other parts of Africa where freedom has been granted," he warned, "the blacks have been unable to govern without the whites, and dictatorship is on the increase. But we are prepared to co-operate with the black states of Africa."

For his Afrikaner audience, the bulk of the speech was a sentimental appeal for the republic that the Nationalists wish to introduce. But even this call was made with an apologetic glance at the English-speaking South African. "We have done everything to honour the monarch," declared the ex-editor who deleted every reference to the 1947 Royal Tour from his paper. "South Africa could become a Republic without leaving the Commonwealth. If the English-speaking community would sacrifice their sentimental attachment to the monarchy, it would remove a factor that prevents all South Africans from becoming united."

Then another appeal to the outside world. "We in South Africa are the best allies the West can have in Africa. We are in the forefront of Western civilization. We are the only consistent and genuine nation on which the West can rely. Do not throw your friends away.

"The Communists are trying to get the support of the coloured nations in Asia and Africa. You won't get that support if you work up a grievance against the white man in

South Africa. This will only help Communists condition the African nations against the West."

It was a tortuous argument—if you criticize South Africa, you only help the Communist cause. The entire speech left the impression of a man who feels misunderstood pleading for support. In contrast to past performances, in which he cocked a snook at the world and offered his opponents the alternative of liking his policies or lumping them, Dr. Verwoerd appeared desperately in need of friends.

He asked for world support, he sought English South Africa's co-operation in forming a republic, and the republic he offered was not the cherished return to the old Boer Republic that Strijdom had preached. The applause at the end was scarcely rousing, and the crowd quickly dispersed after singing the Doxology.

12. BROEDERBOND

ON THE FLIGHT to South Africa one of my companions was Dr. W. T. Ross Flemington, president of Mount Allison University in New Brunswick and a former senior chaplain with the Canadian Army. Dr. Flemington and I went our separate ways inside the Union, each spending about the same time there and each leaving with similar depressing recollections.

"It was like a bad dream," said Dr. Flemington. "I had seen it all happen before when I visited Germany in 1936. The same feeling of fear and uncertainty fills everyone. There are the same mass arrests in the early hours of the morning; the same uncertainty about who will be arrested next; the same terror of the police state.

"Mass extermination may again be the order of the day— but this time it may be of the master race."

Dr. Flemington found the most encouraging signs within the universities, where most of the students and the teaching staff opposed Apartheid. However, even there he detected the cancer of dictatorship among the hard core of Afrikaner teachers who belonged to the secret society called the Broederbond.

Working quite independently of Dr. Flemington, I, too, encountered the Broederbond, which is Afrikaans for union or bond of brothers. Quite possibly, my research into this organization was a factor in my arrest and detention. The Broederbond's membership reaches high into the senior ranks of the police force and right into the Cabinet. The Prime Minister, if not a member, bears the Bond's endorsement, and ten out of fourteen members of the first Nationalist Cabinet were reputed to be Broeders.

In George Orwell's *1984*, a horrifying vision of a super police state, Big Brother was the dictator. His slogan was "Big Brother is watching you," and in the complacent West this was debased into an alleged joke.

In South Africa it isn't funny. Big Brother is all too real and watchful. He is the secret head who watches over the Afrikaner-Broederbond, which in turn polices the morals and politics of the entire Afrikaner community. Remember Fritz Kuhn and his Nazi Bund in the pre-war United States?

The Afrikaner-Broederbond is the secret society for Afrikaners, the descendants of the early Dutch settlers. At one time, membership was restricted to those who went back two generations as South African citizens, a rider that would have debarred the Dutch-born Dr. Verwoerd. The Bond's aim is a Christian Nationalist Calvinist Afrikaner Republic of South Africa, where not only white will be supreme over black, but also the chosen whites—the Afrikaners—will be undisputed rulers.

The Broederbond is not the crude band of ignorant night riders that the Ku Klux Klan is. Bond and Klan share the same repulsive racial theories, but among the poor whites of the Klan there is no one of the intellectual stature of the Broeders who concoct the philosophical foundations for the planned republic. The Bond is strong in the Afrikaner universities, and one of its trinity of Big Brothers was said to have been Dr. J. C. Van Rooyen, a theology professor at the

University of Potchefstroom. This college in the Transvaal is the fountainhead of the Dopper or Nederhuits Hervormde Kerk, the most fundamentalist branch of the Dutch Reformed Church.

The Mafia that strikes terror into the Sicilians, whether they are in their homeland or in the United States underworld, has a certain similarity to the Broederbond. So had the Ustachi, the Nazi Croatian organization that had a brief but bloody sway in Yugoslavia under Hitler's sponsorship.

The Broederbond is more subtle than these other racial-nationalist societies. It is none the less effective in its domination of a greater part of the Afrikaner community.

I smuggled out of South Africa, secreted in a collection of long-playing records of African jazz, photostatic copies of a top-secret report on the activities of the Broederbond that had been prepared for the late Gen. Smuts. After reading this document, Smuts told his own United Party that he wished to make clear his own opinion of this secret society, "because I fear that it holds very serious consequences for the nation, and is going to be the cause of new discord among the people.

"It is clear," said the general, "that the Broederbond is a dangerous, cunning, political, fascist organization of which no civil servant, if he is to retain his loyalty to the State and Administration, can be allowed to be a member."

Public servants were then forbidden by law from joining the Broederbond; but under the Nationalist Government the law has not been enforced, and the civil service, particularly the Ministry of Education, is riddled with Broers.

Although the Special Branch of the South African police seized some of my notes on this report, they missed the photostats themselves. At one stage of my arrest it almost seemed we were playing the childhood game of "hot and cold" as, to my concern, they got nearer to the hidden material and then, to my relief, retreated from it.

"Where did you get your information on the Broederbond?" demanded Captain van der Westhuizen of the Special Branch, during my interrogation. "It is contrary to the code of my profession to reveal sources of information," I replied. If a South African court had asked the same question and received the same reply, I would still be languishing in Durban prison under sentence of contempt.

"Why didn't you ask a member of the Broederbond to explain it to you?" asked the captain in an effort to appear persistent. I gently explained that my researches into the Bond had been interrupted, but that I had been under the impression that this was a secret society and its members were sworn to silence. On second thought, the captain seemed to agree with me.

Although my detention in Durban jail interrupted my investigation, I had been able to complete some cross-checking. More than one source, and each was independent of the other, showed me copies of the top-secret report. It was also satisfying to discover, on my return to Canada, that Dr. Flemington shared my impression of the Broederbond as an active and potentially dangerous group.

I must also report that one of my informants suggested that the Broederbond's power had dwindled until it was no more sinister than the Native Sons of Canada, a group that has been unable to convince the Canadian Government to adopt either a national flag or an anthem. However, this source was very much in the minority, and others who provided information maintained that the Bond was one of the most important factors in South African life.

When Dr. Verwoerd was its editor in 1944, *Die Trans-vaaler*, the Nationalist daily, listed the aims of the Broeder-bond:

—the independence of South Africa;
—the abolition of the inferiority of Afrikaners and their language;
—strict segregation of all non-whites;
—an end to exploitation of South Africa and its people by "aliens";
—rehabilitation of the farming class and social security through more intensive industrialization;
—nationalization of credit, and a planned economy;
—the Afrikanerization of public life and education "in the Christian National sense".

Die Transvaaler also recorded that the Bond acknowledged only "the highest court—the volk itself". The paper also stated the Bond's belief that "the Afrikaner nation is planted in this country by the hand of God, and is destined to exist as a nation in its own right and with its own mission."

Here is how it works today: an upper-middle-class mother of English descent with three children under ten told me her youngsters had a friend their age of Afrikaner stock. One day recently, while visiting the English family, the young Afrikaner suddenly paused and in the hearing of my friend, said: "I've just remembered. I shouldn't be here. My mother told me I shouldn't play with the English."

Is the story familiar? During the early thirties how often were similar words said in Jewish homes by the children of Nazis, or in the southern United States, where white and Negro children play together until some racialist intervenes?

In South Africa, instilling anti-English prejudice into children is only complementary to the main task of inoculating youngsters with the false sense of superiority over anyone whose skin is coloured. The Bond is busy at both tasks. A young Afrikaner falls in love with a girl who is not Afrikaner. The Broederbond steps in to prevent the marriage. If persuasion and appeals to race purity do not work, economic pressure is applied.

South Africa has the most fantastic bureaucracy outside the Iron Curtain countries. It has been estimated that two out of five white South Africans work for the state or state-owned enterprises. If the Afrikaner who wants to marry outside the fold is a teacher or works on the state railway he will be warned he is jeopardizing his chances of promotion. The Bond permeates the bureaucracy and can make or break a state employee's future.

The South African police and armed forces are virtually Afrikaner preserves. And I mean the Apartheid-minded Afrikaner. Let me make clear that all Afrikaners are not bigoted fools convinced that anyone with a black skin is automatically an uncivilized savage and is incapable of being anything else.

The most brilliant exposition of South Africa's problems was given me by a liberal Afrikaner. Unfortunately this type of person is yet another South African minority and a target for Broederbond attack. The Bond reserves a special hatred for non-conforming Afrikaners. Even Gen. Smuts, who believed in segregation, is regarded as a traitor who tried to "Anglicize" the Union.

In its attacks on the use of the English language, the Broederbond has been so successful that in the Afrikaner universities the students' command of English is so poor that those in the scientific faculties find difficulty in understanding their English text-books.

In social life, people whose mother tongue was English said that to maintain contact with the Afrikaner it was necessary to talk to him in Afrikaans. Not so many years ago, the Afrikaner would use English if the Englishman's Afrikaans was not perfect. Now the conversation is in Afrikaans or nothing.

One object of this insistence on Afrikaans in the schools and in private life is the long-term goal of depriving the English-language newspapers of their readership. This now includes mulatto and African people, whose children will not be taught enough English in school for them to read an English paper.

On the basis of what I saw in South Africa and what I was told by responsible people there, the Broederbond follows the same principles and is as active as when Gen. Smuts received this report on March 29, 1944:

> In November, 1935, the late Gen. Hertzog, at the time Prime Minister of South Africa, made public a series of revelations about a sinister secret association, the Afrikaner-Broederbond, hereafter to be referred to as the A.B., about which very few people at the time had even the remotest inkling.
>
> The immediate result of this denunciation was that the organization submerged completely and apparently disappeared from the scene. This was not so. It had merely become more secretive than ever before, but also more active and more dangerous.
>
> In the period since 1935 it has grown enormously in power and has succeeded in establishing concerns and contacts in every sphere of public life in the Union.
>
> The framework for achieving its ultimate object, Afrikaner domination of the Union, has been well and truly laid. With its intricate network of branches and cells, it can "manufacture" public opinion at will in spite of

Government [Gen. Smuts's United Party was then in power] victories at the polls.

The Afrikaner-Broederbond, which is "accountable only to God" for its actions, was founded in 1918 "on the rock of Jesus" with the broad aim of bringing about South Africa's "God-given destiny," a Christian National Calvinistic Afrikaner Republic.

As Gen. Hertzog so significantly pointed out, "Afrikanerdom" in the Afrikaner-Broederbond sense of the word refers only to the Afrikaners who believe in Afrikaner domination of South Africa. All English-speaking South Africans are excluded, as well as Afrikaners who support the United Party as it exists today.

Any form of co-operation with the English-speaking section is frowned upon by the Afrikaner-Broederbond and many prominent members have been ruthlessly blacklisted for being guilty of furthering and approving such co-operation.

To use the words of one of the leading Broers at one of the organization's annual conferences: "The Afrikaner-Broederbond must gain control of everything it can lay its hands on in every walk of life in South Africa. Members must help each other to gain promotion in the civil service or any other fields of activity in which they work, with a view to working themselves up into important administrative positions."

Part of the oath taken on initiation solemnly binds each member "to further the interests and undertakings of fellow Broers"; this is considered to be one of the many types of "Bondsplig" (Bond duty), than which there is nothing more holy and binding.

Prospective candidates, who must not be under twenty-five years of age, are secretly watched and tested for years. They must be men of standing and influence, and members of as many concerns as possible. Prospective members must be proposed by two members with-

out the knowledge of the person concerned. Three
counter votes blackball him.

The initiation: The organization is Masonic down to
the smallest detail. There are the usual three degrees,
with an elaborate ritual of initiation, secret signs of
recognition, grips and passwords for every degree. The
mystic symbol of the Order is *Die Lig van Majuba* (the
light of Majuba, a Boer victory over the British in 1881).

The members speak in confidence *onder die vierkleur*
(under the four-colour, a reference to the old Transvaal
Republic flag), like Masons do "on the square".

The initiation is rather gruesome. In complete darkness a corpse-like body lies on a bier, wrapped in a
black winding sheet on which is embroidered in letters
of blood: *Verrad* (treachery). A bloody dagger is thrust
to the hilt in the body of the "corpse". A torch throws
brief flashes of light on the scene while the chaplain
intones:

"He who betrays the Bond will be destroyed by the
Bond. The Bond never forgives and never forgets. Its
vengeance is swift and sure. Never has a traitor escaped
just punishment."

In cases of serious betrayal, the storm-troop section
of the Ossewa-Brandwag (literally the ox-wagon sen-
tinel, referring to the Great Trek) is detailed to mete
out punishment. The Ossewa-Brandwag is secretly controlled by the Afrikaner-Broederbond.

Although the outward forms of Masonry are slavishly
imitated, its fundamental creed, that all men are
brothers, and its absolute prohibition of politics are con-
spicuously rejected. The Afrikaner-Broederbond is osten-
tatiously religious. There is much psalm singing and
Bible kissing throughout its ritual, but in the eyes of
this esoteric fraternity, the Great Architect of the Uni-
verse has hitherto designed only one model, the *ware
Afrikaner* (genuine Afrikaner).

Precautions of secrecy: No notices, instructions and

so on are ever conveyed through the post. They are delivered verbally or personally. Meetings are always convened under a bogus name. For example, the Vissersaal (normal college) Bloemfontein, the venue of a recent Afrikaner-Broederbond conference, was booked under the pretext of a Student Christian Association conference.

The setup of the Afrikaner-Broederbond:

1. The Trinity: This is the inmost nucleus of the Afrikaner-Broederbond and consists of the Supreme Secret Chief supported by two assessors who are members of the Uitvoerende Raad (Executive Council).

2. The Uitvoerende Raad consists of twelve members known as the Twelve Apostles.

3. The Algemene Raad (General Council): It consists of the Twelve Apostles and numerous "disciples" drawn from the various divisions or cells.

4. Local branches or cells: A cell has five or ten members and a division consists of two or more cells. A division must have a maximum of forty members. Each independent cell or division is responsible to the Uitvoerende Raad.

5. Vigilance committees: Directly responsible to the Uitvoerende Raad. This is the Afrikaner-Broederbond's Gestapo system. Such committees are appointed at various strategic points to guard over and report on Afrikaner-Broederbond-sponsored interests, for example, the Afrikaner Medical Faculty at Pretoria, the Engineering Faculty at Stellenbosch, the South African Railways, etc.

The Afrikaner-Broederbond was formed on May 24, 1918. The original membership amounted to fourteen and has grown since to 2,528.

The Afrikaner-Broederbond's tremendous influence must be attributed to the fact that its policy is based on two fundamental principles, namely to control the minds of Afrikanerdom through control of its educational institutions, and to control its actions by gaining a grip on its purse strings.

In other words, the Afrikaner-Broederbond has, octopus-like, spread its tentacles into the economic, as well as the educational and cultural fields in South Africa. In addition, it has representatives in key positions throughout the civil service.

The Reddingsdaadbond was originally started with the noble object of regenerating the poor whites. Like Hitler's Winter Help, it professes to help the poor, whereas it is in actual fact a purely capitalistic and highly lucrative concern which unscrupulously exploits the needy and gullible for the benefit of a select and powerful few.

Forty per cent of the members of the Afrikaner-Broederbond are either teachers in schools, normal colleges and universities, or predicants and others who are members of bodies controlling teachers and colleges. A list is available of at least five hundred teachers in South Africa who have become members in the last two years.

All teaching posts are secretly canvassed by Afrikaner-Broederbond members, and in the areas where they have the say in various school bodies, nobody not approved by the Broederbond vigilance committee has a ghost of a chance of appointment or promotion.

Gen. Hertzog said: "I know of few towns and villages in the Free State where the Broederbond has not established for itself a nest of five, six or more Broers to serve as a focal point for Bond propaganda, and I know there is hardly a single nest where there isn't at least one teacher sitting as a hatcher. Thus we can form a fair idea of the underground activities carried out by teachers behind the curtains of the school desk.

"Is it right," the General asked, "that teachers should be allowed, through membership in the Broederbond, to declare their hostility toward the English-speaking children entrusted to their care, whose parents help pay their salaries just as well as the Afrikaner children's parents do?"

The police force is one of the special preserves of the Bond. The Bond has its representatives in South Africa's legations, in the Department of Economic Development and Demobilization, in the Treasury, Departments of Social Welfare and Education, in the South African Railways, in the Posts and Telegraph Department, and in the Departments of Agriculture and Justice.

The Ossewa-Brandwag waxed with the rise of Nazi power and waned proportionately with its decline. The Afrikaner-Broederbond will however, unless checked, outlive both, since its policy is far more patient and insidiously clever. If the Afrikaner-Broederbond is not exposed and its stranglehold eradicated root and branch —in particular its insidious hold on education—it will, at its present rate of growth, within a few years destroy South Africa.

Thus did the Nazi system, also starting with a small but powerful underground group, gain ultimate control, dragging the whole world into the most devastating war of all time. The potentialities in the case of South Africa are more dangerous than in Germany. Germany's Nemesis was disguised in the form of a humble and poorly educated house-painter. South Africa's equivalent is a university professor.

Today the Bond controls most of the Afrikaans press. Every community has its *élite* Broers—a few key professional men, important business men, or sports figures—whose function is to further the aims of the Bond and promote the myth of white South Africa.

Is it any wonder that on March 30, 1960, the Government formally turned the country into a police state by the proclamation of Emergency Regulations?

13. POLICE STATE

LIEUT.-COL. GIDEON PIENAAR was the first senior South African police officer I met. He was a tense and worried man. This was three days after the Sharpeville massacre and I was not aware that he had been nominally in command of the frightened constables who had disgraced their calling by shooting unarmed Africans in the back.

Nor did I learn until later that it was Col. Pienaar, fingering a scratch from a stone on his car, who provided an epitaph for Sharpeville's sixty-seven dead: "If they do these things, they must learn their lesson the hard way."

It was my first day in the Union of South Africa, and immediately after my plane landed I had hired a taxi and headed for Sharpeville. We were stopped at the gate and told that entry to the location could be gained only with the permission of the police commandant in Vereeniging. From the police station we were directed to a dingy suite of offices above some shops on the main street. With me was Gerald Clark of the *Montreal Star*.

Clark and I introduced ourselves to two officers and asked how to go about getting permission to visit Sharpeville. The request seemed to stagger them and was instantly refused. A third officer, who turned out to be Pienaar, walked over and tried to explain the situation. He was, he said, in charge of all police in the area. He was slightly built, in his fifties, and obviously under considerable nervous strain.

"Under no circumstances can you go into the location," he said. "The situation is still tense. Just your presence inside might start things all over again. I could not guarantee your safety one minute."

Could we go in with a police escort? No, that was impossible. We simply didn't understand what was happening. "These people are savages," declared the colonel. "You have no idea what they are like. Of course, they have grievances. We all know they have grievances. We want to help them but the agitators have got hold of them. They are Communist agitators. They're stirring them up and causing all the trouble."

Col. Pienaar was almost distraught as he kept trying to impress us with his explanation of a Communist plot. He would not discuss the massacre itself—later he was to tell the official inquiry that while he gave the police the order to load their guns he also gave "specific instructions there was to be no shooting without an order to do so". That order was disobeyed and "at some personal risk" he had jumped in front of the policemen who were firing into the crowd and, waving his arms, called on them to cease fire.

Obviously anxious to escape our questions, the colonel cut short the interview on the excuse that he was already late for another appointment. It was a brief but revealing episode, and what seemed most significant was his desperate urging of the "Communist" explanation for the demonstration.

Clark, who had been in Poznan, Poland, during the 1956 riots there, turned to me outside and said, "I've heard it all before. It was almost word for word the same story that the

Communist police chief in Poznan gave me. Only he blamed everything on capitalist provocateurs."

The fact that Africans, who had for so many years tamely submitted to the police, would now defy authority to the point of stoning constables seemed to upset several long-service officers. One of them almost wept on my shoulder one night after the windshield of his car had been shattered by a well-aimed rock. "I have always been good to them," he said, "and the respectable natives have thanked me for what I have done.

"I never used the sjambok," he went on, pointing to the wicked leather whip hanging behind the police-station door. "I'd never use it more than once every couple of months. I was fair and they respected me. And now this."

Ironically, earlier in the evening before the violence broke, he had been discussing his own teen-age son with me. The boy was now bigger than his father and no longer amenable to parental discipline. "What do I do?" he had asked. "The boy is too big for me to spank any more."

As I poured him a teacup of brandy to steady his nerves after the stoning (and I needed one myself), I did not have the heart to point out to this veteran policeman that there was perhaps a parallel between the son who had grown up and no longer obeyed his father and the Africans who had also been treated like children. Perhaps the Africans had grown up and it would take more than whips and bullets to keep them in their appointed place.

The third police officer I encountered was Col. J. C. Lemmer, Johannesburg's elderly and crotchety chief of police. Col. Lemmer, who was slightly hard of hearing, had his headquarters in a block of offices known as "The Greys". During the emergency it was his custom to hold press conferences four times a day. These meetings were so unproductive of news that one night I found myself and Stephen Barber of the *London News Chronicle* the only ones there.

It was 7 P.M., March 30, the day when the Emergency Regulations had been proclaimed and the police had made their first early-morning swoop, arresting nearly five hundred people without warrant or charge. Col. Lemmer, who had held two earlier press conferences, said he had no further news for us.

"Would you care to comment on the arrest of Chief Luthuli?" I asked. "I understand that his counsel complained in court today that Chief Luthuli was assaulted in prison shortly after his arrest today."

"That is a lie," Col. Lemmer declared. "Luthuli was not in court today and he was not assaulted. No one would be stupid enough to hit Luthuli. He's too popular. You can take it from me that this never happened."

By this time the colonel was glaring at me, his face pressed as close to mine as it could get. Not having the details of Chief Luthuli's complaint with me, I dropped that subject and asked the colonel if it were true, as reported in the Supreme Court by the distinguished barrister, I. A. Maisels, Q.C., that he had been served with an order to appear before Mr. Justice Ludorf and that he had chosen not to appear.

Col. Lemmer denied having been summoned to the court. He had been in his office, he said, but he had not been served with any order.

Barber and I left this barren session and dropped in at the offices of the *Rand Daily Mail,* where we heard a rumour that some detainees were being released at Marshall Square police station. Outside the station we asked a young sergeant whether it was true. "Yes," he replied, "they're being re-leased and rearrested. Everything's upside down today."

We waited and nothing happened; we went inside to find the duty officer and the most senior policeman. He was a young Afrikaner sergeant with a shaven bullet head, looking like a fugitive from the Hitler Jugend, and he could not talk to us. It was back to Col. Lemmer, six or eight blocks away at "The Greys".

"Is it correct," Barber asked, "that some of the prisoners at Marshall Square are being released?"

"You don't know if there are any detainees at Marshall Square," replied the colonel. "And I don't have to tell you. I can hold them wherever I like. As far as you know, I may have released them already."

We agreed with the police chief's oblique answer, and tried to explain to him that we were only trying to establish the facts. He made it plain that he was equally interested in keeping them from us, delighting in his new powers under the Emergency Regulations. Then Barber dropped the bomb.

"You realize, sir," he began, "that you misinformed us about Chief Luthuli. He was in Mr. Justice Rumpff's court at Pretoria today, and he did complain through his counsel that he had been struck by a prison warder. Probably an honest error on your part."

That did it. Col. Lemmer became apoplectic. He accused Barber of trying to quarrel with him. "What's your name?" he demanded.

"Stephen Barber of the *News Chronicle*."

"Get out of my office," shouted the colonel. "You, Mr. Stephen, can no longer come to my press conferences. You [pointing to me] can come to my press conferences." He slammed the door.

About fifteen minutes later, I thought of the parting thrust I should have made.

While recounting this incident to some South African colleagues, I tried to make the point that the function of a police chief was to serve the public and not, as Col. Lemmer had done, try to conceal information. The South Africans told me to calm down. "We're inoculated against that sort of thing," one said. "It happens here all the time. The police think they are a law unto themselves."

Under the Emergency Regulations, the South African police did become a law unto themselves. Trying to explain the situation to its readers, the *Johannesburg Star* stated:

> South Africa is virtually under martial law. All of several Johannesburg lawyers agreed on this—the only difference being that the country is under police control, instead of military control, which it would be if martial law was declared.
>
> "These regulations obviate any necessity for the Government to impose martial law; South Africa will now have to face the realities of life in a police state," was the opinion of one.
>
> Another lawyer described the new regulations as having all the powers of the sweeping War Measures Act, under which almost anything could be done in the interests of national security. "There is little that cannot be done under this Act by the police," he said.

The Public Safety Act empowered the Government to declare a state of emergency, at its own discretion, and then govern by decree. The Minister of Justice was authorized under such circumstances to exercise unlimited powers of control over everybody and everything. Contrary to similar legislation in other countries, no time limit was imposed to guard against the Executive's assuming these vast powers when the need was not present.

In South Africa these emergency powers are not confined to the Government or to the Minister of Justice. Some are shared with magistrates and commissioned police officers. The Act allows "arrest without warrant and detention of people whose detention is, in the opinion of the Minister of Justice or a magistrate or a commissioned officer of the police, desirable in the interests of public order or safety or of the person concerned, or for the termination of a state of emergency".

Habeas corpus was suspended and arrests under the Emergency Regulations did not need to be followed by an appearance in court. If the person arrested was detained for more than thirty days, within another fourteen days the Minister of Justice was required to table his name in Parliament, if Parliament was sitting or when it next assembled.

Once a person was arrested no one was allowed to disclose his name without written permission from the Minister. A wife might not whisper to a relative that her husband was detained. The penalty was $1,400 or five years, and the same punishment faced anyone who refused to answer lawful questions; but what a lawful question was, and whether it demanded answers that might be self-incriminating, was not defined.

The regulations also empowered officers named by the minister to investigate any association which was in any way related to the state of emergency, to summon any person before them, make him swear to tell the truth, and question him.

It was made a crime to print or to be caused to be printed,

to distribute or to circulate, to utter or display, any "subversive statement." This was defined as any statement "calculated or likely" to have the effect of (a) subverting the authority of the Government or of the Legislature; (b) inciting the public or any person to resist or oppose any minister or official or members of the police or military forces in any measure connected with the safety of the public or the maintenance of law and order; (c) engendering or aggravating feelings of hostility towards any section of the public, class of persons, or person; (d) causing panic, alarm, or fear among the public, or weakening the confidence of the public in the successful termination of the state of emergency, "unless the statement is proved to be a true and complete narrative". Under this section a prosecution must be initiated by the Attorney-General and, it was assumed, heard by a court of law.

But individual detainees were not allowed to see legal advisers. In a test case in Durban, my future cellmate, Dr. Michael Kenneth Hathorn, was refused access to lawyers and relatives by Mr. Justice Henochsberg, who ruled that since it was for the Minister of Justice to determine when, where, and how a person was to be detained, it must follow that the manner of his detention was an executive matter "in which this court cannot interfere".

Contrariwise, Mr. Justice Galgut in Supreme Court, Pretoria, ruled it was the fundamental right of every South African citizen, upon apprehension or arrest, to obtain legal advice and consult with his legal advisers. However, his ruling only applied to five detainees whose relatives had made application to his court. Nearly two thousand other detainees went without this "fundamental right".

Liberties won in centuries of struggle were tossed overboard overnight. To add to the tenseness of the situation, the South African Broadcasting Corporation began reading out long lists of men being called up. The entire European able-bodied population with any kind of military training was commandeered to service to "prevent or suppress internal disorders in the country".

Mobilization began the day that Emergency Regulations were proclaimed, and affected 175 commando units (56,800 officers and men), a Citizens' Active Force (reserve or national guard formation) of about 50,000, and the army, whose exact strength was made a secret but which recent statistics showed to include 1,275 officers and 7,744 men.

Most important were the police, numbering 28,137, half of whom were non-white. Organized on a national basis, they could be flown from one part of the country to another whenever trouble threatened or when a show of force was to be made. For example, police from the Rand were imported to Cape Town for the brutal campaign of "intimidating the intimidators" that involved beating up Africans and mulattos at random in the city's shopping districts.

The first hint that the police were to be unleashed through the proclamation of Emergency Regulations came on March 29, when Governor-General Charles Robberts Swart made a flying trip between Cape Town and Pretoria. An ardent Republican and Nationalist, Mr. Swart was Minister of Justice when the Public Safety Act was passed giving the Governor-General power to proclaim an emergency and rule by decree.

Mr. Swart—"Blackie" to his friends—was once a bit player in Hollywood Westerns, and later a high-ranking officer in the Ossewa-Brandwag, the Broederbond's strong-arm section that actively attempted to hamstring the Union's contribution to World War II. As a child, Mr. Swart was interned during the Boer War in a British concentration camp, an experience that, understandably, left him anti-British and an extraordinary choice as the Queen's personal representative in South Africa.

Six feet six inches tall, the Governor-General once cut an imposing figure striding into the House of Assembly armed with a cat-o'-nine-tails. He was Minister of Justice at the time and responsible for a bill making flogging obligatory for certain offences. (The 1958 figures show 93,775 strokes inflicted, including 17,223 on juveniles, or nearly double the 1952 figure of 760 strokes for white, 206 for Indians, and for Africans and mulattos 49,111.) Mr. Swart has been at pains since to explain that when he brandished the cat in Parliament, he was merely demonstrating the humanity of his method of corporal punishment by cane.

The Governor-General's contribution to the crisis was signing the Emergency Regulations proclamation. But before the Regulations became law, it was necessary for them to be printed in the official *Gazette,* published in Cape Town. Either through ignorance of this fact or through over-eagerness, the South African police jumped the gun on the morning of March 30.

In Johannesburg at five minutes after two that morning, lawyer John Lang and his wife Brenda Betty were awakened by rapping on the glass panel of their front door. Lang got up to investigate. One of the visitors identified himself as Inspector Swart of the Special Branch, and said he had come to arrest John Lang.

"Where is your warrant?" asked the lawyer.

"We don't need a warrant under this Act," replied Swart.

"But the Act hasn't come into force."

"Don't worry," was the arrogant answer, "it will be proclaimed by the time it's required."

Lang, of course, was right; the police all over the Union were exceeding their authority by making arrests before the Regulations had been promulgated. Mrs. Lang acted quickly, and by 7:15 A.M. her application for a writ of habeas corpus was delivered to Mr. Justice Ludorf, who ordered Lang produced in Supreme Court by 10 A.M.

The police did not produce Lang. Neither did Col. Lemmer, Johannesburg's Chief of Police, nor Col. Att Spengler, head of the Special Branch in the Rand, heed the court's summons to appear; although Lemmer did send his lawyer, Mr. Van Wyck de Vries. At 11:15 A.M., Lang was finally brought to court in the custody of a Capt. Willers, who wouldn't let his prisoner speak to the lawyer representing him.

For the police, Mr. de Vries claimed a state of emergency existed, but he could offer no proof to the judge. Finally, at noon Mr. Justice Ludorf ordered an urgent telephone call to the Prime Minister in Cape Town, to try to find out the true state of affairs and whether his court had any jurisdiction.

Dr. Verwoerd was at a Cabinet meeting. In reply to the judge's question, he admitted that he did not know whether the Emergency Regulations were in force, but he promised to find out. A second call was made to the Prime Minister but it could not be completed.

In this incredible situation, Mr. Justice Ludorf ruled that the police had failed to establish their case, and he ordered Lang released, with costs against Col. Lemmer, the senior officer at Marshall Square police station, and the senior officer of the Security Branch.

Back stage, the police worked frantically to justify themselves. Someone had the bright idea of sending a copy of the *Gazette* containing the Emergency Regulations by wirephoto from Cape Town to Johannesburg. Meanwhile relatives of other detainees were applying to the court for writs of habeas corpus, and the judge was granting them.

The police lawyer asked for an adjournment to permit the transmission of the photostats. Shortly after 5 P.M. a police officer dashed into the courtroom and handed a packet to Mr. de Vries. He looked at the contents and shamefacedly addressed the court: "The photostats are the wrong ones. They are of another *Gazette* that was published in Cape Town today. I apologize for inadvertently misleading the court and ask to be excused. I will not oppose the release of the applicants."

It was 1:20 A.M. the following morning, or nearly twenty-four hours after the arrests, that the South African police force eventually managed to place a copy of the *Gazette* before Mr. Justice Ludorf. The messenger was the head of the police Special Branch, Col. Sampie Prinsloo.

Deliberately flouting the court order that called for the release of detainees whose relatives had secured writs of habeas corpus, the police held on to their prisoners until after 7 P.M. Col. Spengler then organized a farcical performance whereby the detainees were taken from their cells at Marshall Square and led to the charge office. There they were solemnly released at one end of a desk and then passed along the counter, where they were re-arrested.

A few days later the wife of one of the detainees, a mother of a three-month-old child, asked her lawyers to take action that would allow her to see her husband. The lawyer, James Kantor, went to see Col. Lemmer and for his pains was warned by the police chief that mention of the detainee's name in an affidavit might result in police action against the firm of attorneys under the Emergency Regulations.

In her affidavit, the applicant said she had been "advised against stating the relationship between her and the person detained". She referred to him as "your petitioner's relative".

Another case, reported by *The Observer* in London, involved the arrest of "Mrs. Gegrude Cohn, who has had no involvement in politics, presumably instead of her husband with a similar name, Mr. Gerard Cohn, who is Transvaal secretary of the Liberal Party; there is thought to be no way of appealing this error."

This was the police state, the name, as Rebecca West said, given to the corpse of a state. Its top man was the Commissioner of South African Police, a thin-lipped, hard-eyed political policeman, Major-General C. I. Rademeyer.

Gen. Rademeyer virtually ran South Africa for a time after the unfortunate assassination attempt on Prime Minister Verwoerd. (On this occasion, the Prime Minister's bodyguard, a South African police officer, fainted dead away.) Before the shooting attempt, the General enjoyed the unusual power of reporting directly to Dr. Verwoerd, going over the head of his nominal superior, Justice Minister Frans Erasmus.

Erasmus revealed how the general kept him in ignorance on several occasions. Once, at a press conference, the Justice Minister admitted he was unaware that Chief Luthuli had been arrested. On other occasions, Members of Parliament asking Erasmus privately about people detained discovered the Minister himself knew nothing about the cases concerned, and himself suggested inquiries should be directed to Rademeyer.

It was obvious that it was the police chief and his senior assistants who decided who should be arrested under the Emergency Regulations; and it was the Minister of Justice who heard about them—or some of them—much later.

Rademeyer had the bright idea, some months prior to the 1960 crisis, of sending a team of his officers to Algeria, where the French for five years had been at war with a native population. There the South Africans learned the technique called in French *ratissage,* involving the surrounding of a village and the systematic beating up of its inhabitants.

Renamed *kragdadigheit,* this brutal method was applied by Rademeyer in Cape Town and, in particular, at the African suburb of Nyanga. It was my reporting of these events that led Rademeyer to send his Special Branch men after me.

Rademeyer was a Broederbond man and linked closely with extremists in the Nationalist Party. He was fond of sitting in Parliament watching the debates, and once called in for questioning an Opposition M.P. who had forecast that Dr. Verwoerd would not be Prime Minister after April 20.

After the Prime Minister was wounded, Rademeyer teamed up with extremist Nationalists, and it took a full Cabinet meeting to call him to order. His enjoyment of police-state power ended less than a month after the Emergency Regulations were imposed. It was announced April 29 that the general was retiring as the result of a "sudden illness".

14. THE AGONY OF NYANGA

CAPE TOWN lies like a half moon at the foot of Table Mountain; from the summit can be seen the Indian and Atlantic Oceans as well as the magnificent city. Living there are 729,200 people including 286,200 whites, 362,400 mulattos or Coloured, 9,900 Asians, and 70,700 Africans.

The Africans live in locations—foul Windermere, still one of the world's most revolting slums; Langa; Nyanga; and a few smaller suburbs. The newest, cleared from sandy waste land two years ago, are Langa and Nyanga, each with about 25,000 residents. They live in municipally built houses, row on row of two-, three-, and four-roomed dwellings, plus some barrack-like buildings for single men.

The single men are not necessarily unmarried; many of them have come from the reserves to find work. These workers are welcome in the white man's city; they man the docks more efficiently than the mulattos and at a quarter the price. But their wives and children must remain in the Ciskei or the Transkei, so they may develop independently, according to the laws of Apartheid.

Cape Town has been proud of its "liberal" racial attitudes, looking askance at the other cities—Johannesburg, Durban, Port Elizabeth, and East London, where the cauldron was continually boiling over into riots and demonstrations. Cape Town with its apolitical Coloured majority seemed to be above violence. That was until 1960, to be precise March 21, the day chosen by Robert Sobukwe, president of the Pan-Africanist Congress, for a demonstration against the pass laws.

Sobukwe had organized well, using the Pan-Africanist technique whereby each leader trained an understudy. No one had paid him much heed; the Government, the police, the press, and even the few white South Africans sympathetic to the African cause, all regarded Sobukwe's movement as just another splinter group from the African National Congress. It would fizzle and expire. This was another example of the white South African's failure to understand the black South African. In Cape Town the Africans listened to Sobukwe and liked what they heard.

At 7 A.M. Monday, March 21, nobody went to work from Langa or Nyanga. And at Langa police station two thousand people gathered in response to Sobukwe's call, while fifteen hundred rallied outside police headquarters in Nyanga. The P.A.C. leader had told them to leave their pass books at home, then go quietly to ask the police to arrest them for breaking the pass laws.

At Langa the crowd swelled to about five thousand. At their head was a most remarkable young man, Philip Kgosana, a twenty-one-year-old student at the University of Cape Town. Kgosana came from the Transvaal, where his father was a small farmer, to study commerce and finance. He was one of the last Africans to be admitted to this white university, and to surrender his career represented real sacrifice. Still he left the campus to become one of Sobukwe's disciples.

Kgosana was a short, slender, intense youngster whose face and hands communicated the African's agony under

Apartheid. Yet his whole troubled face frequently broke into African good humour. His boyishness was accented by the short pants he wore and the faded blue sweater. This is his story of March 21:

> We gathered at the Langa single quarters and we decided to move to the police station. We were approached by a group of armed police. I had an impression that they were about to carry out a baton charge. I immediately left my followers—about five thousand of them—behind and went to the police. I told the police that I was the man responsible for the demonstration and I asked to be arrested.
>
> The senior officer in charge of the police refused to arrest me. He wanted to know who would control the demonstrators while I was in jail. I told him that our demonstration was opposed to any form of violence. The police then wanted to know what our plans were. I told them we were marching to the police station where we wanted to be locked up for being without our passes. The senior officer told me that if we went anywhere near the police station he would defend the station to the last bullet and to the last drop of blood.
>
> As I am against violence, I asked my people to disperse. I told the officer I would withhold my labour and I asked him to withhold his bullets. I then picketed the police station, and kept the demonstrators away from the police station.

Police Captain W. Louw said that he saw Kgosana chasing away Africans from the police station and heard the young man repeatedly declare: "I will not allow the police to be attacked. I will protect them with my life."

Later, Captain Louw led a patrol into the location and tried to break up a gathering of Africans near the bachelor quarters. There was no Kgosana and stones and bottles began to fly. Louw claimed to see shots being fired from a window so he ordered his men to open fire. They killed one man outright and mortally wounded two others.

Langa went mad that night and in a frenzy of fury burned its schools, churches, library, and administrative buildings. The destruction weighed most heavily on the Africans themselves, but the buildings went up in flames as symbols of white authority. The next day thousands from Nyanga and Langa stayed home from work. Those who did go in to their city jobs were approached by Pan-Africanists who told them to quit immediately. Irresponsible elements joined in, uninvited, and one gang known as "The Spoilers" was reported in Cape Town intimidating Africans still at work.

Thursday, March 24, the police struck back. They invaded Langa, beating up anyone encountered, trying to force workers into buses and trains going to the city. Those who did submit to the police and went to work were visited by organizers and packed off home. By noon Cape Town was emptied of its African labour force.

Kgosana appeared the next day, when he led fifteen hundred men from Langa into Cape Town's police station in Caledon Square. When the fifteen hundred demanded to be arrested for being without passes, the city's harassed police chief, Col. I. P. S. Terblanche, said, "I have no time to demand reference books at this stage." Again Kgosana led his followers away without any show of violence.

The police made their next move the following Wednesday, March 30, when the Emergency Regulations were imposed and arrests could be made without warrant or charge. At a hurried meeting Kgosana and his Pan-Africanist colleagues decide to make a protest march to Parliament and demand the release of their leaders. By noon they were on their way from Langa and Nyanga, a column more than a mile long. Inside the city, other Africans who had travelled by train waited to meet the marchers in Buitenkant Street outside the Caledon Square Police Station.

Church bells tolled an alarm for the first time since the abolition of slavery. And on came the marchers, thirty abreast, thirty thousand strong, led by Kgosana striding along in his short pants. He stopped the throng on De Waal Drive leading into the city and warned them, "I appeal to you for non-violence. We must avoid bloodshed at all costs."

As they moved forward again, they broke into song:

> Our burden is heavy
> And it needs strong men to make our boat—
> A boat like Noah's boat.
> Let us make this boat an ark made out of Africa.

A South African Air Force helicopter buzzed angrily overhead. Army troop carriers and armoured cars raced through the streets of Cape Town to throw up a cordon around Parliament. Inside the House of Assembly the Prime Minister maintained, "The position is completely under control," while in the Senate the fatuous Minister for Bantu Affairs, De Wet Nel, solemnly declared that race relations had never been better; only 1 per cent of the Bantu supported all the present goings-on; the other 99 per cent were delighted with the Government.

Col. Terblanche emerged from the besieged Caledon Square police station and spoke for six minutes, urging European and Coloured spectators to move away. He ordered all businesses in the vicinity to close down. The vast African crowd parted silently to allow four three-ton trucks loaded with armed police to pass through their ranks. Then the marchers arrived and Buitenkant Street was jammed from side to side with one solid mass of Africans.

Kgosana was borne to the forefront of the demonstration on the shoulders of three of his supporters. A white police officer held a loudspeaker for him. "Let us be silent," he began, "just like people who are going to the graveyard." And a hush fell over the multitude of men, women, and children.

"This morning," Kgosana went on, "the police came into Langa and threw the people out of their homes to force them to go to work. So we have come here to ask the police for protection. Our leaders have been arrested and without them we are a body without a head. Only the leaders can stop the people from violence, and without the leaders, the Africans might not be peaceful."

The words of the twenty-one-year-old student filtered back through the mass of people. He told them that he had spoken with Col. Terblanche and had received an assurance that the police would not molest them on their way home. Col. Terblanche had also guaranteed that a small deputation, led by Kgosana, would be given an opportunity to see the Minister of Justice and present a protest to him.

"We have made our protest," Kgosana concluded. "Now let us return peacefully to our homes."

Under the strange power of their student leader, the crowd began to disperse. Some marched in a body back towards Langa with a police car leading the way. Others drifted away from the city centre in small groups. It was a most moving demonstration of Gandhi's non-violent method of peaceful protest by thirty thousand Africans and their youthful leader. Col. Terblanche also deserved credit on this occasion for the restraint of his police forces. Not a single weapon was used.

Dr. Verwoerd's contribution to the day's events was the

statement that, if African demonstrations became more violent, greater force would be used to hold them back and, if necessary, the army would be called in. "The government will not hesitate for one moment to take every step necessary to control the situation," he declared. "I want to put people's minds at rest."

The Prime Minister and his police chief, Gen. Rademeyer, lost no time in answering the Cape Town demonstration with a show of force. The same night, under cover of darkness, thousands of heavily armed sailors and soldiers surrounded Langa and Nyanga. The two African suburbs were sealed off from the outside world. Two planeloads of armed police— the toughest bullyboys—were flown from Johannesburg to Cape Town.

As dawn broke on Thursday an air force helicopter hovered over the beleaguered locations broadcasting instructions for the Africans to return to their jobs in Cape Town. They were given until 7:30 A.M. to catch trains or buses to the city. Then the cordon was closed and no one allowed in or out.

Justice Minister Erasmus announced he would "honour" the police promise, that he would receive a delegation in his own peculiar way. Mr. Erasmus would not condescend to see Kgosana and his colleagues, but he would see that they were received by the Secretary for Justice, C. J. Greeff.

Kgosana went to the meeting with Greeff, whether as a free man or as a prisoner was not known. But Kgosana was not seen again by his followers. The Justice Department's sense of "honour" had no qualms about arresting Kgosana under the Emergency Regulations. Whatever the Justice Department thought, there were sixty thousand Africans who regarded this act as a betrayal.

The people of Langa and Nyanga had only one way of

expressing their feelings effectively. They stayed home from work, continuing the strike that had begun on March 21. Food supplies were running low; Africans have no savings to tide them over a period of unemployment, and if they did not work there was no money for groceries. The Liberal Party began sending in bulk food—mostly corn meal—and the Africans organized their own rationing scheme for its distribution.

On Friday April 1, the Government-controlled South African Broadcasting Corporation reported on its evening newscast that the situation in Cape Town was quiet. With the exception of an incident at Hermanus, where police baton-charged three hundred Africans, all was calm. There was no mention of Mrs. Beatrice Manjati's baby, who lay dead with its brains blown out.

This was the story of Beatrice Manjati: Beatrice and her husband Samuel were Africans living in Nyanga. Perhaps it was hunger that made their eighteen-month-old child cry all night, but Nyanga's one doctor advised the parents to take the baby to the Red Cross Children's Hospital in Cape Town. This required a car, and the parents found a friend who would drive them. In African fashion, Beatrice Manjati strapped her infant on her back and got into the automobile.

It was about 9:30 A.M.—two hours after the location had been cordoned off for the day—that the car reached the Klipfontein Road exit to Nyanga, and was stopped by sailors manning the barricade. The driver asked permission to take his passengers to hospital. Permission was curtly refused. The driver asked if he could back up. According to his wife, who was in the car, this permission was given and he began backing into the location.

A shot was fired. Rev. Stanley Qabasi, of Holy Cross Anglican Church, Nyanga, said the bullet killed the child instantly and lodged in the mother's shoulder. Neither the police nor the Defence Force would deny the shooting; neither would accept responsibility for issuing a statement explaining whether this was an accident or not. But there was no doubting the effect of the incident on the people of Nyanga. They stayed on strike.

The police explanation for the continuation of the strike was a simple one. "Agitators" and "intimidators" were preventing the law-abiding Africans from going to their jobs. There may have been some truth to this theory; unions and political movements usually have their enthusiasts whose task is to drum up activity by the rank and file. In addition irresponsible, gangster elements among the Africans were undoubtedly rising to fill the vacuum caused by the arrest of moderate leaders. The "agitator" hypothesis may have had some truth, but it was not the whole truth behind the passive resistance of Langa and Nyanga.

General Rademeyer's boys who had been to Algeria believed the time was right for *ratissage*, wholesale beating up of the two African locations. Governor-General Swart quickly signed new amendments to the Emergency Regulations giving troops and police power to use force, including force resulting in death, to remove or prevent suspected trouble.

"Under the new regulations," explained Col. Terblanche, "natives who cannot account for themselves in the city streets and other areas where they might cause trouble, can be dealt with on the spot. Force must be used to get those potential trouble makers and intimidators off the streets."

Monday, April 4, was D-day for the new terror campaign. Apartheid's brutish nature was flaunted openly on the streets of Cape Town for all to see, including diplomats and foreign correspondents. I was walking down Darling Street in the main shopping centre, when I noticed passers-by had stopped to stare in one direction. I followed their glances to see ten policemen armed with sjamboks, or whips, chasing three Africans and beating them at the same time.

Telephone calls began jamming newspaper switchboards. One man told of watching police beating Africans outside Maitland police station. "I could not stand their screaming," he said. A Goodwood town councillor complained when he saw police whipping Coloured men outside a liquor store, and a police sergeant told him it was being done on instructions.

Patrick Duncan, editor of the Liberal Party paper *Contact*, and the son of a former governor-general, tried to intervene when he saw a policeman attack an African. For his pains, a police sergeant told Duncan he would be arrested for interfering with the course of "justice".

On Adderley Street, one of the city's finest thoroughfares, an African clergyman was standing peacefully in his clerical garb. A policeman approached him demanding, "Where do you work?" When the man replied, "I am a clergyman," the constable attacked him with his sjambok and chased him down the street.

Another victim was an African articled clerk waiting outside the magistrate's court for a copy of a court record, when he was set upon by half a dozen policemen.

On a street in the suburb of Rondebosch, Dr. A. C. Jordan, a dignified man of fifty-two and a lecturer in Bantu languages at the University of Capetown, was stopped by a loutish, teen-aged white policeman. Dr. Jordan was smoking a cigarette. The constable slapped it out of his hand, ordering him not to smoke while talking to a white man. He frisked the doctor insultingly, and then slapped his face before marching him to the police station.

So flagrant was the conduct of the police that C. F. Regnier, President of the Cape Chamber of Industries, went to Col. Terblanche and pleaded with him not to continue the assaults on law-abiding African and Coloured workers.

In the Parliament buildings, politically minded General Rademeyer smugly told an Opposition member, "We are intimidating the intimidators."

Shocking as the police violence was on the streets of Cape Town, it could not equal the calculated viciousness of their assault on the cordoned-off suburb of Nyanga. At 11 A.M. police squads were turned loose inside the location with orders to whip every male African they encountered. They broke into houses to flog men in their beds. Terrified, screaming wives and children watched their husbands being dragged out into the streets.

Whips and batons ruled Nyanga. The hospital clinic was closed down, leaving only one doctor to minister to the wounded. African nurses made frantic calls to Cape Town for supplies of bandages and first-aid equipment. As further punishment, water supplies to the surrounding locations were cut off; but, strangely, the police overlooked disconnecting the few telephones. And so reports of the barbaric police raids trickled out.

Other reports of the grisly campaign inside Nyanga were brought out by Africans who had gone back to work. No newspaperman was allowed in to watch the Day of the Whips, as the police sought to instil so much fear into the unarmed Africans that they would never again dare to demonstrate against Apartheid.

Four Africans were wounded on Monday. At least five, including a seven-year-old child, were injured by police bullets on Tuesday. Fourteen Anglican clergymen appealed to the Government to restrain its use of force. "We therefore in the name of God urge the Government to exercise more wisely and moderately the powers they have taken to themselves to deal with the emergency."

At Nyanga the awful purge was continued through its third day on Wednesday. Unbelievably, the African spirit had showed little sign of wilting. No leaders were left, and one of the last telephone calls that I listened to was a pathetic plea, "We don't know where to look for guidance."

For sheer sadism, the closest comparison to what happened at Nyanga was when the Gestapo sealed off the Warsaw ghetto and began to annihilate it. Had Nyanga fought back, it, too, would have been wiped out; but the Africans employed non-aggressive tactics that puzzled the police. It was not until the fourth day that they were able to claim success. By that time I was nearly a thousand miles away in Durban, but I felt that I should try to write an epitaph for these courageous people of Nyanga, a name, ironically, that in Zulu means "to heal" or "to make well":

> The agony of Nyanga is over. The South African police force yesterday climaxed their four-day reign of terror over this African suburb of Cape Town, seizing 1,525 of its residents and driving them two miles to a police station for screening. They later detained 162.
>
> When I spoke by telephone to the *Star's* Cape Town correspondent yesterday morning, he said: "It's torture, sheer torture. They are lining people up inside Nyanga and beating them."
>
> Nyanga's ordeal began three weeks ago. It has been an impressive piece of passive resistance, protesting the rigid pass laws, police shooting and the arrests of African

leaders. An unconscious tribute to Nyanga's prolonged non-violent demonstrations was paid by Cape Town's police chief. Although his forces claimed to have seized a vast assortment of weapons, Deputy Commissioner Terblanche states that the "natives" had offered no resistance during yesterday's mass invasion.

What is the real lesson of Nyanga? Nyanga has demonstrated to the world the real meaning of Apartheid. The sadism of the police bullyboys has been exposed. . . . Nyanga stripped the sham pretence from Dr. Verwoerd's claim to be "a Christian with a conscience". I watched him sit bland and composed in Parliament, twiddling his thumbs while his police were deliberately flailing unresisting Africans.

Nyanga was the lie-detector test for Verwoerd's Justice Minister Frans Erasmus, boldly telling Parliament that police were forbidden to use whips, the sjamboks they wielded on Cape Town's streets and which I have seen ready for use on the back of a police-station door.

Nyanga was also the crucible for the official Opposition United Party. It sat silent in Parliament, making no protest.

Nyanga may appear quiet today and the average South African may feel assured that the trouble is over with the arrest of the "agitators". The Africans may appear submissive, but it would be a fool who thought South Africa's problems had been solved. The arrests mean that there are about two hundred families left in Nyanga without a breadwinner. What will happen to these women and children? And the hundreds who suffered police bullets, whips and batons?

Their wounds may heal, but in the future will it be possible for their leaders to hold them to a course of non-violence?

15. PARLIAMENT

IN ITS fifty years' history the Union of South Africa has created parliamentary traditions that have done their best to withstand the assault of twelve years of Nationalist rule. There is also a legalistic attitude among the Nationalists that compelled them to go through the parliamentary motions even during the state of emergency, when they had power to rule by decree. Parliament thus became, during the emergency, the one forum where free speech could still be practised.

"There will be no more freedom of speech in six weeks' time," (when Parliament was due to adjourn) Mrs. Helen Suzman warned the House of Assembly early in April. Under the Emergency Regulations, it was the only place where people could say what they thought and freely propagate their beliefs.

Mrs. Suzman was one of the group of twelve members of the Progressive Party that took full advantage of their rights and duty of opposing the Government. In fact, the Progressives were the opposition while the official Opposition, the United Party, abdicated its responsibilities and voted with the Nationalists during the crisis. Or, as they say in South Africa, the United Party moved into the white man's laager with the Nats.

When the Government decided to outlaw the African National Congress and the Pan-Africanist Congress, it introduced the Unlawful Organizations Act. The Leader of the Opposition, Sir de Villiers Graaff of the United Party, ripped the measure to shreds, attacking the Government's insatiable appetite for more and more arbitrary powers. He then came to the remarkable conclusion that his party would vote for the bill because "we want to be generous to the Government and give it any powers it wants to maintain law and order".

It was left to the leader of the Progressives, Dr. Jan Steytler, to say to both Government and Opposition, "You speak of maintaining law and order. But what sort of law and what sort of order?"

The Progressives were all elected as members of the United Party, but in August, 1959, they broke away from Sir de Villiers' ineffective leadership. The new party was formed in November, with a program considerably more liberal than that of the United Party but not quite as liberal as the Liberal Party. Their aim was to call a halt to racial war and plan for peaceful racial co-existence.

The Progressives would repeal the Population Register Act, which labels every citizen according to race; the Group Areas Act, which decrees residential segregation; the Immorality Act, prohibiting sexual relations between whites and non-whites; and the Extension of University Education Act, barring non-whites from white universities and relegating them to tribal colleges.

The right to vote would be extended to non-whites of a certain educational standard (as yet undetermined). A commission has been appointed to examine the possibility of racial groups being represented in a reformed Senate where they would have veto powers.

The platform also calls for abolition of the pass laws and

"influx control" (barring Africans from the cities), the relaxation of industrial colour bars, and the granting of trade-union rights with some government supervision.

The Progressive Party program is a considerable advance on the United Party plan. Sir de Villiers would give full voting rights back to the Coloured people but would restrict Africans to a choice of white members who would represent their interests in Parliament. The United Party would abolish race classification but it would retain pass laws, influx control, and the Group Areas Act. Execution of these Apartheid measures would be carried out less harshly than under the Nationalists.

With the United Party cuddled up inside the white man's laager with the Nationalists, the Progressive Party was preaching the only alternative to Apartheid heard in Parliament. (The Liberal Party was not able to elect any members.)

The Nationalists enjoyed possession of 103 seats in the 150-seat Assembly. Each man reputedly was hand-picked by Dr. Verwoerd on the basis of personal loyalty, and an unlovely crew they made. While the Prime Minister and some of his Cabinet observed the niceties of Parliamentary debate, Ministers like De Wet Nel and many backbenchers were vituperative and frequently calculatedly rude when Opposition women members were speaking.

In his selection process, Dr. Verwoerd managed to include such wild men as Dr. Carel de Wet who, before the Sharpeville death toll was announced, called for greater force and declared he was disturbed that "when there are riots by whites or non-whites only one should be shot". Another professional know-nothing named Vorster, of all things the Deputy Minister of Education, made his mark forty-eight hours before the imposition of Emergency Regulations by assuring the House, "The fact is there is no emergency in South Africa."

Parliament lived up to its traditions when the delightfully cantankerous Professor Sakkies Fourie rose from the kitchen, as the Independents' seats are called. He, too, broke with the United Party, but sits alone because he has been unable to convert the Progressives to his republican creed.

"The Government thinks that it can save the whites by way of *baasskap*," Prof. Fourie said in one of his scourging speeches. "*Baasskap* in the second half of the twentieth century! *Baasskap* can't be limited to the non-whites alone—it is already being more and more imposed on the whites. No more than you can divide liberty, can you divide *baasskap*. The price of *baasskap* over the non-whites is *baasskap* over the whites."

Fourie earned the nickname of Parliament's intellectual sjambok, and he whipped out all around him, scorning the pusillanimous attitude of Sir de Villiers in failing to vote against the Banning Bill. "You cannot ban ideas," warned the waspish professor. Then, as a parting shot to the Government's accusations against "agitators", he declared, "We've become agitator-mad. Don't we know the history of our own people? Every time a man has stood for a truth, he has been stamped an agitator."

While Professor Fourie held the floor—and he spoke in Afrikaans—the Government benches were silent as scolded schoolchildren. They recovered their valour whenever Mrs. Margaret Ballinger rose. She was the lone Liberal in the House, not elected as a Liberal, but voted into Parliament as one of the "Natives' Representatives," white people chosen as spokesmen for the African population. There were seven of them—three in the Assembly and four in the Senate—to speak for nearly ten million Africans.

Mrs. Ballinger was a sincere, white-haired woman, forthright of speech and dedicated to her constituents' interests. Her outlook was liberal and she would have been an ornament to any Parliament. When the Government announced imposition of Emergency Regulations and unleashing of its police force, Mrs. Ballinger stood in the House and said: "I regard this as quite the most tragic day in my political experience.

"The present situation goes a great deal beyond the provision of force. Something more is needed to reassure the people. What happens after force has been used? That is the question I want answered."

According to Mrs. Ballinger, the cause of the crisis was the lack of political and economic opportunity for the Africans and the poverty that went with it. The situation was worsened by the appalling blindness of Nationalists like G. F. von L. Froneman, who said that the Government had 99 per cent of the Africans behind it.

"The fact is," declared Mrs. Ballinger, "that nobody knows where the African population stands—only that from time to time it is bursting into riots. What is important, though, is that the Government should have some constructive policy. As it is, its program is not only driving the Africans to despair, but every white who is prepared to fight for the rights of the Africans now finds himself under the same menace."

In her Parliamentary office, Mrs. Ballinger told me: "I don't know whether I want to see into the future. Evidently, a section of the Africans want to carry on strike action, but I don't know whether they have enough strength and organization to force the Government to recognize them.

"My own feeling," she continued, "is that they should take what they have won up until now. Up to this point they have focussed attention on genuine grievances and they have shown the country that unless these grievances are remedied there is bound to be serious trouble. I have known of these grievances but I have never been able to make a political impact with them. It has never been possible for people like myself to get changes made within a reasonable time. The reason is that Europeans are not really touched by the pressures under which the non-Europeans live. Our economy is so strong—the rake-off is so good—that even the commercial and industrial people, who know they would be better off if the African got a better break, don't do much to get reasonable policies adopted."

Mrs. Suzman, the vivacious Progressive Party M.P., put this lack of contact between white and black on a kitchen level. "I give my African servants orders in English," she said. "They talk together in what to me is a foreign tongue. I have no idea what they are thinking about me, about white people, about anything."

Other white South Africans tried to make an unfunny joke of this communication barrier. "My servants would never take a knife to me—they'd only kill the people next door."

Another M.P. said, off the record, "Emotionally, I am a South African. If the whites here have something coming to them, if there's going to be a bloody revolt, I feel I should stay and take it. If I guided my actions by logic alone, I would sell up immediately and leave."

It was the wife of another Progressive Party member who explained to me how the communications barrier is erected.

I shall not mention her name, for there were laws in the mad world of Apartheid under which she could be banned from receiving Africans in her home; and she was one of the few white South Africans who extended hospitality to non-Europeans.

This woman came from an upper-middle-class English-speaking family, and she confessed to me that whenever she shook the hand of a black man, she had to overcome a feeling of repugnance. It was illogical, emotional, and she knew it was wrong, but the reaction had been drilled into her. The culprit probably was her white nanny, who conditioned her charges by warning them not to go near Africans, because if they touched one some of the black would come off.

Fantastic, yet an important factor in Apartheid. And believable in a land where the Government fired all the Negro and mulatto employees in the Parliament buildings in the interests of white supremacy.

The Nationalist Party controlled Parliament. First, the system of representation gave more weight to the rural constituencies, and enabled the Nationalists with 50 per cent of the vote, to capture two-thirds of the seats. Then Strijdom had packed the Senate and the Appeal Court to make sure that they would be subservient and not try to rule any Apartheid legislation unconstitutional. At the height of the 1960 crisis, the United Party further obliged by voting with the Government. What need was there for the Nationalists to think of forming a coalition administration?

Some time in the future Japie Basson's National Union Movement might be able to draw enough members from the Nationalist and United Parties to become an effective group. Basson's program was full co-operation between English and Afrikaans-speaking communities; republican government within the Commonwealth; for the Coloured, the right to elect their own representatives to Parliament; for the Africans, the right to be represented by whites, large-scale development of the reserves, and consideration for the African city dweller.

There was scarcely anything in the National Union manifesto that would not have met with the approval of the late Gen. Hertzog, the father of Apartheid. The platform represented a return to traditional Nationalism, and by contrast was a marked advance on the sterile Verwoerdian doctrine of Apartheid by force.

Basson was counting on weaning away perhaps as many as thirty government M.P.'s who inclined towards moderation. The remainder of his support would come if and when the United Party disintegrated into right and left wings, the more liberal element joining the Progressive Party.

Dr. Zach de Beer, Chairman of the Progressives National Executive, could see the United Party trying to outbid the Nationalists for the vote of the reactionary whites who wanted "to keep the Kaffir in his place". According to Dr. de Beer, the Progressives were offering the only real alternative to Nationalism. The question was whether there was still time left for the racial situation to be given the moderate treatment advanced by the Progressives. And could the Progressives win enough seats in their first appearance at the polls, should an election be called before the 1963 deadline?

As for Mrs. Ballinger, there was for her no future in Parliament. The white supremacists silenced her by abolishing the Natives' Representatives and unseating the present ones as of the end of 1960. To all intents and purposes, inside Parliament, the Nationalists, with their two-thirds majorities in both Houses, had made South Africa a one-party state.

Abolition of the Natives' Representatives also meant the loss of a Parliamentary forum for the Liberal party and its plan for a multi-racial state. The Liberals look eventually to the adoption of a universal franchise, but believe this may have to be reached by a transitional stage, during which the vote might be granted subject to educational qualifications. Their goal was an end to Apartheid and full democratic government.

"This goal," said Liberal Chairman Alan Paton, "may be reached in one of two ways, either as an aftermath of violence and revolution resulting in black racial domination, or by an evolutionary process of a massive kind. I do not know one Liberal who believes that change will come about as a result of steady and quiet evolution."

16. ARREST

IT WAS NOT necessary to go to prison in South Africa to get a close view of Apartheid, but Durban jail did offer a post-graduate course in the practical application of racialist theories.

For three and a half days—seventy-nine hours and twenty minutes, to be precise—I was an inmate of Durban jail— prisoner 7019/60. According to South Africa's Minister for External Affairs, Eric Hendrik Louw, I wasn't arrested at all, I was only "held for questioning". He made quite a thing out of this distinction, the niceties of which escaped me during my sojourn from April 9 until April 12 in the Durban lockup. In fact, the interrogation on April 11 lasted a scant fifteen minutes and was nothing more than a farcical attempt to cover up the blunder of my imprisonment.

Jailing me only advertised South Africa's descent to the status of a police state where freedom of the press was dead and civil liberties forgotten. My own predicament was a brief, if harrowing, experience, but it gave emphasis to South Africa's tragic internal conditions.

My term in jail served better than anything I could write to rouse the attention of the outside world to what was happening in the land of Apartheid. And it may have opened the eyes of a few South Africans who had let traditional liberties be destroyed without making much protest.

A few days after the imposition of Emergency Regulations, Mr. Justice Henochsberg ruled in Durban that in his judgment "the ordinary law affecting the liberty of the subject has been abrogated". Commenting on this, the *Cape Argus* of Cape Town added, "In other words, for the time being and as long as the state of emergency lasts, South Africans are no longer a free people. It is at the absolute discretion of the Minister to determine when, where, and how a person is to be detained. With the freedom of the citizen goes much of the freedom of the press."

That freedom of the press no longer existed was obvious to foreign correspondents working in South Africa. While South African newspapers continued to praise Major-General Rademeyer and his South African police force, it was a foreign correspondent, my colleague Robert Nielsen of the *Toronto Star,* who revealed that Rademeyer kept his nominal superior, the Minister of Justice, in ignorance and for a time was virtual ruler of a police state. Other correspondents, including myself, reported the calculated police brutality and its effect on the African population. When our dispatches were cabled back to South Africa by Reuters, the Emergency Regulations prevented South African editors from reprinting them.

Not long before my arrest I discussed press freedom with a leading South African editor. "This is a dirty question," I said, "because I'm not sticking my neck out. But shouldn't you be sticking your neck out farther? You haven't told your readers, for example, the full story of Nyanga and the deliberate policy of beating the Africans into submission."

"This has been worrying us," the editor explained. "The board of directors has discussed it and their decision was that it would be better to carry on as we do, going as far as we feel we can, rather than go all out and find ourselves banned—out of business. But for myself, I think the time is fast approaching when I'll have to face the choice of martyrdom. And that will be the only honest course."

In my own case, there was no conscious choice of whether or not to court imprisonment. My assignment was to report what was happening in South Africa and I did just that. In a country such as Russia where there is open press censorship, a foreign correspondent sometimes faces the choice of including or leaving out information that he believes the censor will not pass. He does not know whether the censor will simply delete the section or suppress the entire report. Some times it is advisable to wait until you have left the country before writing a critical article that would not pass censorship and might result in the correspondent's expulsion.

South Africa had no formal press censorship. It was obvious from the reports of commissions investigating the state of the press that the Government kept dossiers on foreign correspondents, and I had no doubt that some official had the task of making a collection of my dispatches. There were also suggestions, in the Afrikaans papers supporting the Government, that censorship should be imposed. *Die Vaderland* of Johannesburg said, the day before my arrest, that steps might be taken to eliminate the anomaly of a free foreign press operating in the same emergency areas as the South African press, on whom limitations had been placed. (Obviously *Die Vaderland* had not yet received the Nationalist party line from Mr. Louw that the Government had never taken any steps that could be construed as against the freedom of the press.)

Dr. Verwoerd himself was squeamish about admitting interference with press messages. Some hours after his Government or his police had suppressed entirely my last dispatch on Nyanga (without advising me), the Prime Minister was asked whether it was his intention to impose press censorship in respect to the actions of the police and Citizens' Force units. Dr. Verwoerd's reply, read for him in his absence from Parliament, was that the Government would take whatever steps it deemed necessary from time to time.

There were three possible explanations for my arrest without warrant or charge:

1. A warning to all foreign correspondents and a threat to their sources of information.

2. A vindictive action revealing the jittery state of the white-supremacy Government and the dominant position of its national police chief, General Rademeyer.

3. Because of the investigation I had commenced into the sinister secret society—the Afrikaner-Broederbond.

The timing and content of my last report on Nyanga was also relevant. The police had been unleashed on the streets of Cape Town and inside Nyanga on Monday, April 4. The Government and Gen. Rademeyer had not taken into consideration world reaction to their brazen brutality. South Africa received a bad press in the overseas newspapers Tuesday and Wednesday. "In the horror of Nyanga are kindled fresh fires of hate," said the *London Daily Mail*. Its correspondent Peter Younghusband, a quiet giant of a South African, had written: "For two days this place has been the scene of a relentless and violent campaign of terror. If I had been told a fortnight ago that this would have happened in this country, and perpetrated by my fellow-countrymen, I would never have believed it."

These reports, mine included, filtered back to the South African Government on Wednesday and Thursday. On Friday, Mr. Louw, in his capacity as head of the South African Government Information Service, was stung into attacking foreign correspondents for sending "wildly exaggerated and in many cases completely untrue reports to their newspapers and agencies". His case was somewhat weakened by the fact that the Government had refused to allow Members of Parliament to visit Nyanga and investigate what the police had been doing.

On top of this came my summing up of the significance of Nyanga. According to Mr. Louw, the clerk in Durban Post Office who accepted it from me on Friday morning was so horrified by its contents that he turned it over to the Ministry of Justice. Said Mr. Louw, the report by Phillips was "absolutely untrue".

Gen. Rademeyer and the Government decided to teach me a lesson. Not until my second day in jail did I learn that they had seized and suppressed the cable that outraged them.

The first inkling I had of their displeasure was at ten minutes after seven, Saturday morning, April 9. There was a knock on the door of my bedroom in Durban's Edward Hotel. When I opened the door in pyjamas and dressing-gown, I found an assistant manager who said apologetically, "These gentlemen wish to see you."

The gentlemen were two obvious plain-clothes policemen. "Mr. Phillips?" asked the senior of the two. When I nodded, he said formally: "I have come to arrest you under the Emergency Regulations." His name was Head Constable M. H. Wessels and he was accompanied by Det. Sgt. M. C. Swart. They entered my room. There was nothing I could do to stop them; under the Emergency Regulations, the victim has no right to know what he is accused of and no right to legal advice or access to the courts.

I asked Wessels for his identification (which he produced) and to be allowed to communicate with the Canadian High Commissioner. He said the High Commissioner would be notified in due course and ordered me to dress and pack my bags. While I put on my clothes, Wessels sat at my desk, reading the story in my typewriter. Swart busied himself with a collection of pamphlets describing aspects of Apartheid. Almost as an afterthought, Wessels inquired if I had any firearms. He accepted my word that I did not carry any weapons.

My breakfast arrived, and my visitors urged me to eat it while they probed my files and belongings. Occasionally they would exchange remarks in Afrikaans which I could not understand, but there was obvious satisfaction in their tone as they bundled up books and papers.

Swart went through my suitcase and found a paper package. With exaggerated courtesy, he asked me to unseal it and show him the contents. It contained examples of Zulu beadwork that I had bought as a souvenir for my daughter. "Tourist junk," Swart sneered, dropping the beads with distaste.

Newspapers and newspaper clippings did not seem to interest them, but they pounced eagerly on books and pamphlets. I could almost see them licking their lips when they found one slim volume, *The Anatomy of South African Misery* by Dr. Cornelius de Kiewiet, President of the University of Rochester, New York. I had bought it the previous day in Durban's leading bookstore; but the detectives shook their heads over what they patently considered its subversive nature.

I asked for a receipt for the pamphlets, notes, and papers they were seizing. "You're the best typist," Swart replied.

"You type it out and we'll sign it." I asked what I should do about my luggage. Didn't I have a friend in Durban who would look after it for me? Swart suggested. I certainly wasn't going to embarrass any South African citizen by involving him with the police. I reminded the sergeant that I had arrived in Durban only the day before and had no friends there.

On our way out of the hotel, my captors insisted that I stop and pay my bill. I made use of this opportunity to delay my departure in the hope that some other correspondent might see my predicament. None appeared; but word of my arrest did get to Canadian Broadcasting Corporation correspondent Donald Gordon, who was first to notify the Canadian High Commissioner of my arrest.

I asked the hall porter if I could get some cigarettes. With a gesture of sympathy he offered me one from his own pack, while sending a bellboy out to purchase some for me. Swart then motioned me to get in his grey Volkswagen while Wessels entered another, driven by a uniformed man. I had been warned previously never to drive in a Volkswagen through an African location. To the African, they are a symbol of the hated Police Special Branch and I would be apt to be mistaken for a policeman.

The drive was less than half a mile. With heavy-handed Afrikaner humour that I scarcely appreciated, Swart said: "You chose your hotel well. It is very convenient to the jail." Durban jail was built by British colonial authorities about sixty years ago. Its exterior, cream with green trim, was not particularly forbidding, and I had previously driven past without noticing it.

What was ominous was the slip of paper Wessels produced as he rang for the doors to open. Addressed to the

Governor, Col. D. B. McLachlan, it said: "Receive the body of Norman Phillips, to be held under the Emergency Regulations for as long as the Minister (of Justice) decides." I did not hear the iron doors shut behind me, nor was I conscious of bolts being shot home or keys turning in massive locks. But burned in my memory was that one phrase, "the body of Norman Phillips".

A few minutes later the body received a number: 7019/60. *Verhoorafwagtende* (awaiting trial), said the three-inch-square ticket that was the body's passport or claim check. *Naam:* Norman; *Alias:* Phillips; *Beskuldiging* (charge): Emergency Regulations; *Opgeneeem* (admitted): 9-4-60. The body's thumbprint was pressed on the reverse side, where the word *gaol* was misspelled *goal*. The body was relieved of property, pens, money, watch, and bow tie. It was led through two sets of bolted and padlocked iron gates to Cell Block A.

17. JAIL AND AFTER

THE MEN'S SECTION of Durban jail consisted of five cell blocks—two-story buildings, each with a maximum of thirty-six cells. While I was an inmate the number of prisoners varied between sixteen hundred and nineteen hundred. Of these, there were never more than one hundred whites. The score was chalked up daily on a notice board just inside the jail doors, and it gave the prisoners some diversion to try to guess the daily totals.

Block A held white prisoners only. We were accommodated one to three in a cell. This left approximately 144 cells for fifteen hundred to nineteen hundred Indian, Negro, and mulatto prisoners. Apartheid prevented me from entering the non-white cell blocks, but it was a fair assumption that whatever were the conditions for the whites, those for the non-Europeans were ten times worse.

Cell No. 1, to which my body was consigned, was the resting place of Dr. Michael Hathorn, a brilliant, thirty-eight-year-old medical research worker, and Errol Shanley, a book-maker's clerk. They had been jailed without charge under the Emergency Regulations on March 30, ten days before my arrival. In the generosity of their welcome, once they realized I was a Canadian, I felt less like a body and more like a person again.

Hathorn and Shanley were Durban's only two political

prisoners. A third, a lawyer named Arenstein, had been arrested in the first wave when the over-anxious police jumped the gun. Released on a writ of habeas corpus, he skipped the country before the Special Branch got around to re-arresting detainees. From the time they had been seized, Hathorn and Shanley had been denied access to lawyers; they could not write to their families or receive messages from them. (These petty restrictions have since been eased slightly.) The only communication from their wives came in the form of clothing.

Mike Hathorn spent his birthday in prison, a few days before my arrival. His wife was allowed to send him a package of clothes, with a note on which she was permitted to write "Happy Birthday" but nothing else. What affected him most was being cut off from news of his family of three children, including a three-month-old son.

Errol Shanley also had three children, and on his forty-ninth birthday they each wrote their names on the outside of a parcel of clothes. The clothes were a size too small, but Shanley was not allowed to send them back to be exchanged; that would constitute sending a message, and might imperil the safety of the State. Unlike Mrs. Hathorn, who had a full-time job, Mrs. Shanley could hold only part-time employment, and Errol was concerned about the family income and how their schoolmates would treat his children.

For the treason-trial spectacle, Shanley and his wife were arrested in December, 1956, leaving their youngsters without father or mother. They were released during the first year of this action that, four years later, is still limping through the courts. But, as a direct result of their arrest, their seven-year-old son developed a stutter from which he had just begun to recover. (There were nineteen white children orphaned by the arrest of both their parents under the Emergency Regulations.)

Michael and Errol at first were suspicious of me. The prison grapevine had warned them of my arrival almost as soon as I stepped inside the jail. They, of course, did not recognize me, and their first reaction was to suspect me of being a police spy. My pronounced Canadian accent decided them to accept me, and we became good friends. Actually, I was dependent on them for such essentials as soap, toilet paper, and the few extra food items they had been able to obtain. The best the inefficient police state could do for me was supply three blankets, a filthy pillow, and a soiled linen towel, wet from previous use.

Mr. Louw proclaimed to the world that I had been offered a cot to sleep in, but that I rejected it so that I could say I had slept on the floor. This was as accurate as many of Mr. Louw's statements. I was given no choice at all during my first twenty-four hours, and slept perforce with a felt mat, less than half an inch thick, between me and the concrete floor. After the arrival of the Canadian High Commissioner's representative, I was offered a cot in a separate cell. Since we were allowed out of the cells only two hours in twenty-four, this was tantamount to solitary confinement. I chose the company of my two cellmates and asked for a foam-rubber mattress at my expense, but I was released before this was purchased for me.

Cell No. 1 was seven feet by ten feet; the ceiling arched to a height of twelve feet. The walls were thirty-two inches thick, painted dark grey for about four feet from the floor, then finished in a shade of cream. The floor was red waxed concrete. About six feet from the ground a barred and mesh-screened window, about four by one and a half feet, let in light, air, and sand. Ventilation was poor, and Michael had developed asthma that was serious enough for the prison doctor to give him two pills nightly to permit him to breathe more easily and get some sleep.

A greater threat was typhoid. Durban prison had suffered an epidemic of this disease four months previously, and sixteen prisoners had died. As a doctor, Michael recognized the danger and asked for typhoid inoculations, but these had not been given by the time I was released. However, white prisoners recently had been supplied with plastic bowls and mugs as a protection against infection; non-white prisoners ate from rusty tins.

The governor, a jovial Afrikaner despite his Scots name of McLachlan, used fear of infection to deny my request for food to be sent in from a hotel. He would allow only tinned food, because the jail had only one entrance. Its British architect in 1900 had failed to foresee the imposition of Apartheid, and at Durban all colours passed through the same entrance. Col. McLachlan painted an awesome picture of the germs brought in by prisoners from the dreadful African slum called Cato Manor.

Day began in Durban jail at 6 A.M. with the beating of a triangle. The weak bulb that illuminated our cell was turned on. We folded our blankets and waited to be released into the yard, where we could scrub ourselves and the encrusted dishes from the previous evening's meal. The exercise yard—thirty-five laps equalled one mile—also contained an ablution room and a doorless lavatory with the strange device: "Please leave this place as you would like to find it."

The lavatory was our news centre, as we pieced together the squares of newspaper provided. Only political prisoners were not allowed to read papers; African prisoners, otherwise treated with utmost contempt, were nevertheless allowed their daily newspaper. Our other sources of information were the white criminals, who delighted in breaking regulations by passing on scraps of news.

Meals started with breakfast of mealie pap—a corn-meal porridge without milk—a hunk of bread, and a mug of alleged coffee. Lunch at 11:30 A.M. was another hunk of bread, a grease-laden swill called soup, and a beverage that aspired to be tea.

Supper might come as early as 3:30 P.M. and was either stew or ground meat, potato, mealie rice, and cabbage boiled to an unbelievable streaky brown, plus two slices of bread and margarine. Beverage: a remote derivative of coffee. This was the sustenance for the master race. What the food for non-whites was like, I could only surmise. They were served at the double and, presumably, trotted back to their crowded quarters to eat.

After supper was slopped into our bowls, we were ordered to remove our shoes and leave them outside the cell while we were locked inside until 6 A.M., a stretch of fourteen hours. With us were the dirty supper dishes, natural goal for insects. Our shoes were counted by the warders and then divided by two to reach the number of inmates. From what we could hear, the necessary arithmetic was occasionally something of a problem.

Lights went out at 8 P.M. without warning. Minus our watches, it became a nice problem of judgment when to make up our "beds". Time passed slowly and we could hear the bells on the post-office clock only after traffic had died down. Watches are taken away from criminal prisoners so that they cannot be used for barter; but we agreed that the only excuse for taking them away from political detainees was the added humiliation.

We had no contact with the African prisoners, although at night we would hear keening from African women in their section of the prison, and the weird, deep-voiced cry of an African in solitary confinement, calling on who knows whom, until his voice was suddenly silenced.

The assault on the white prisoners' dignity was a pin-prick compared to the treatment of the non-Europeans. They were left standing naked in the reception room waiting for prison garb to be issued, and they were regularly forced to strip on their return to the prison from work parties sent out into the city during the day. They wore floppy canvas shorts, loose red T shirts, and dirty white jackets. As each gang returned to prison either a white or an African warder searched them for contraband.

The search was a humiliating custom, including the "Tausa Dance" that *Drum* magazine exposed at Johannesburg. Each prisoner stripped off all his clothes and handed them to a warder, who ran his hands over the garments and threw them to the ground. While naked, the prisoner executed the frog-like jig step to show that nothing was concealed on his person. Arms overhead, mouth open, they pirouetted under the bored warder's gaze.

On my first day I was shocked to see that fully half the African prisoners bore the mark of lashes on their buttocks. The weals formed a light patch an inch or two wide against the brown skin. Whippings were administered with the victim strapped to an iron triangle. The weapon was a "light cane", and to add to the exquisiteness of the torture the interval between blows was deliberately stretched out. Accord-

ing to a sailor who had been flogged just prior to my arrival,
the pause before the next stroke was the worst of the mental
punishment, while the pain lingered over twenty-four hours.

About a quarter of a million people a year are jailed in
South Africa, and more than 90,000 strokes of the cane administered. The vast majority are Africans—in Durban the ratio
was more than twenty Negroes to every white man in jail.
For the average African living in an urban area the chances
of being arrested during a year are one in five. One out of
every twenty Africans is arrested annually for breaking the
curfew or failing to produce a pass.

The racialists consider their crowded jails a means of holding down the Africans. In my experience, the jails are sim-
mering pots where hatred of all white people is instilled into
the Africans. Few white South Africans understand this.
Brought up from childhood to consider themselves superior
to black-skinned people, they are insensitive to the indig-
nities imposed on the Africans.

My first day in prison was the worst. Fully twenty-two of
the twenty-four hours were spent inside the cell. There was
no furniture with the exception of crudely made stools on
which we stored our belongings, and we spent our time lying,
sitting or squatting on the concrete floor. For the first few
hours after my introduction to prison food I was in fear of
disgracing myself by retching. It was a combination of the
greasy soup and the nervous reaction from loss of liberty.
Sensing my uneasiness, the doctor, Mike Hathorn, asked me
to talk to them about Canadian history and geography.

My mind lost its power of concentration. There was a copy
of Boswell's *London Journal*, courtesy of the prison library,
but I could scarcely read a paragraph without finding myself

straying into useless speculation: Had the police informed the High Commissioner? What other correspondents had been arrested?

The police had my notebooks and address lists. Would any of the people whose names appeared there be compromised? Some I had met, but many were merely names that had been suggested to me as sources of information. One of the names was Dr. Yussuf Daddoo, an Indian physician who had been a classmate of my family doctor at Edinburgh University. The two doctors had not met since, and when my doctor learned I was going to South Africa he suggested I look up Daddoo. The opportunity did not present itself and I have yet to meet Dr. Daddoo. However, this did not stop Mr. Louw from claiming that I had an appointment with the doctor, and that he was a Communist.

Sleep was impossible the first night as I tossed on the cold cement floor, trying to find a rational explanation for the day's events. My cellmates had initiated me into the most comfortable posture for sleep—lying on the right side with the right leg straight, the left leg bent and the body inclined half-way to a face-downward position—but it was of no help to me, and it was not until my third night on the floor that I managed any sleep.

Had I but known it, I was by no means a forgotten prisoner. Canadian High Commissioner James Hurley and his two senior aides, Gordon Brown and Ross Francis, were active on my behalf in Johannesburg, Cape Town, and Pretoria. Canadian Prime Minister John Diefenbaker warned the South African Government that my arrest could not but add to the wide-spread indignation already felt in Canada at the measures that had given rise to recent violence and loss of life in South Africa.

While Mr. Hurley was *en route* from Johannesburg to Cape Town, Gordon Brown obtained permission from the Government for Ross Francis to fly to Durban to see me. J. P. Hogue, President of the Canadian Daily Newspapers Association, cabled Mr. Louw: "I would express concern and alarm over the reported arrest of an accredited Canadian newspaperman, Norman Phillips. Current Phillips despatches to Canada would indicate that Phillips has observed the best traditions of a free press in reporting facts as he has observed them, without prejudice. His arrest is a startling negation of freedom of reporting as generally understood within the Commonwealth of Nations."

Charles H. Peters, President of the Canadian Press, cabled Mr. Louw: "In the interests of the right to report international news without interference, the Canadian Press, the news association of Canada's daily newspapers, protests the detention of Norman Phillips while in the course of his work as a reporter for a free press, and strongly urges his release without delay."

By then it must have been dawning on Mr. Louw and Gen. Rademeyer that the precipitate action of my arrest was having consequences that they had not taken into consideration. However, Mr. Louw had never been very skilled with the crystal ball. In July 1940, he was the man who declared "General Smuts must give way for a Nationalist Government and the next day we shall negotiate with Germany and Italy for peace."

While Mr. Hurley was making Canada's representations to Mr. Louw in no uncertain terms on Sunday, April 10, I was making my own protest in Durban jail. I had been kept in complete ignorance of the efforts being made on my behalf, and I renewed my demand as a Canadian citizen to communicate with the Canadian High Commissioner. This brought the offhand admission from the deputy governor that fifteen hours ago, the High Commissioner's office had been in communication with the jail regarding my situation. It was typical of the police state that this reassuring news had been kept from me.

Ross Francis then arrived and I was marched into the Governor's office to meet him. Col. McLachlan and his deputy sat at their desks. "Go ahead and talk to him," the colonel told Mr. Francis, "but remember you may discuss only family affairs. There must be no discussion of Mr. Phillips' arrest." Francis stared coldly at the colonel and rose to leave. If this was the way in which the South African Government honoured its word to Canada, he would have no part of it. The Canadian Government had been promised a private interview with Mr. Phillips, with no conditions attached.

The flustered governor said he would have to seek new instructions from Pretoria, four hundred miles away. I was led back to my cell. When the new instructions came, Francis and I were allowed to talk in private, and I learned for the first time of Mr. Louw's theory that I was being held for questioning. It was a considerable relief to learn what was being done to secure my release.

Col. McLachlan was now most solicitous about my comfort. I was to be allowed to purchase tinned food from the canteen daily. (Previously political prisoners ordered canteen goods on Sunday and received them on Wednesday.) The colonel meant well but his orders were not carried out, and the food I ordered that Sunday did not come until Tuesday.

Sunday passed with no sign of the promised interrogation. While I now felt confident of my release, I kept trying to imagine the questions that would be asked and the replies I would give. To distract me, my cellmates regaled me with tales about our fellow inmates. The husky blond giant was in for stealing the car of Durban's chief of police. It took the force a couple of days before they recovered the car. Another convict wore chains on his ankles; he had tried to escape. With the chains he was supplied with "fancy pants"—trousers with ties instead of seams, so that he could remove them for a shower without having to be unchained. Another prisoner had obtained access to the medical supplies and was in the habit of going off on ether jags, achieving a pleasant state of intoxication by inhaling fumes from the anaesthetic.

My interrogation finally took place on Monday, two days after my arrest. The officer in charge was Captain S. J. van der Westhuizen, Chief of the Port Natal Security Branch. He was accompanied by Head Constable Wessels, who had arrested me, but was now acting in the role of stenographer. The time was noon and it was one of the most ludicrous situations in which I have ever been placed. I venture to say that Van der Westhuizen and Wessels would agree.

I asked for a lawyer. The captain, who was ill at ease, said he didn't think I'd need one. Wouldn't I try one or two questions. I explained that the code of the newspaper profession forbade me from disclosing the sources of my information, but that I would hear their questions.

The first queries concerned Bishop Reeves of Johannesburg and Chief Luthuli of the African National Congress. Had I met them? There seemed no point in denying this. Wessels was sitting there with a duplicate of the stories I had written about both men. How many people had I met in Johannesburg? I thought about a hundred. Who were they? I could not tell them. We went over my itinerary and the same questions were asked about each stopping place.

Towards the end, my interrogators were supplying their own answers: "You can't tell us because of the oath of your profession?" I agreed.

At one point the Captain endeavoured to lecture me on how to report events in South Africa. "Why," he asked, "do you get all your information from the wrong people?" I pointed out that my notebooks contained the names of government information officers and police chiefs, from whom I had had refusals of information, turn-downs of requests to interview ministers, and, in the case of Col. Lemmer, misinformation.

"Where did you get your information about the Broederbond?" I could not reveal this. "But why didn't you ask a member of the Broederbond?" I explained that my researches into this group had only begun, but that I had been informed it was a secret society without benefit of public-relations officer. However, if they could introduce me to a Broer, I would welcome the opportunity of interviewing him.

The most fascinating question was a test of my journalistic skill. The chief of the Security Branch wanted to know what I would do if a man came around a corner and told me that a hundred people had died in a fire. This one really puzzled me, but I did my best to explain how a reporter covers a fire and gets his information by observation, and by talking to firemen and other eyewitnesses.

Wessels' few questions were more practical. He wanted me to decipher my notes for him. What did A M and F M radio mean? I explained for him that under his Government's Apartheid program, it had been decided to segregate broadcasts for whites from those for Africans. Those for the black people would be broadcast on the established A M system; those for the whites were in future to be broadcast by F M, or frequency modulation, so that they could not be heard by the radio sets owned by the Africans.

I am sure it was Capt. van der Westhuizen's first encounter with a foreign correspondent and, at first, he seemed as apprehensive of me as I was of him. After fifteen minutes we were both feeling rather embarrassed by having to go through this meaningless questioning for the sole purpose of justifying Mr. Louw's statement that I was held for questioning. The captain terminated the interview on an apologetic note. "You know," he said, "we know less about you than you know about us."

Another twenty-six hours were to pass before I was released from custody. My most vivid memory of my last day in jail was being led through a group of about thirty African prisoners who were squatting in the prison yard. I was in the charge of a warder wearing sergeant's stripes. In his right-hand trouser pocket he carried a short baton to which a leather thong was attached. As he strode through the ranks of the Africans, the sergeant absent-mindedly twirled the leather thong, flicking the squatting men on heads and shoulders. It reminded me of someone strolling through a field of daisies, carelessly lopping off the heads of the flowers with a cane. The sergeant's use of the thong could not be called blows; they inflicted no physical pain, but they cut deep into human dignity.

Half an hour before my release on Tuesday, the extra food that I had been permitted to order on Sunday finally arrived. My birthday fell on the following Saturday, and I left the two tins of bully beef and one of gooseberry jam with my cellmates, Errol and Michael. They promised to save one tin for a celebration on my birthday. What impressed me most about both of them was their pride in South Africa; when I suggested that they come to Canada with their families, they said, "No, this is our country and we are going to stick it out until it is a place where all men can live in peace."

Both Errol and Michael assured me that they knew of no offence they had committed that would justify their arrest. The only explanation for their detention was that their names appeared on a police list; in Errol's case this would have been the result of his arrest and clearance in the treason trial. We went over the list of as many of the detainees as we knew; and Errol and Michael said many of the names were those of people long inactive politically.

One Johannesburg detainee, Louis Joffe, had been an invalid for fifteen years. A contemporary of Mahatma Gandhi, Nana Sita, was in his seventies and had been ill for some time. One Pretoria detainee was under treatment for tuberculosis; a Durban man was badly crippled by arthritis. In Cape Town, the second wave of arrests included a grandmother who had been caring for her son's children after his detention in the first swoop.

The Government eventually announced that charges would be made against the detainees when the police completed their investigations. In the case of Chief Luthuli, he was accused of inciting Africans to destroy their passes. This was understandable in view of the calculated risk he took when he publicly burned his pass. But it will be interesting to note how many of the approximately eighteen hundred political prisoners can be charged with such specific acts, and how many were detained simply because the Security Police disliked their political views.

The other remarkable aspect of the arrests under the Emergency Regulations was that for the first time leaders of the Liberal Party were jailed. These included Dr. Colin Lang, a Pretoria doctor whose patients included several members of the Canadian diplomatic mission. The notable exception was Alan Paton, the Liberal chairman and distinguished novelist. Paton, undoubtedly saved by his international standing, apologized for not being jailed and added, "I must be slipping." The Liberals stand for a multi-racial South Africa, but are dedicated to achieving that goal only by constitutional means.

One explanation for the arrests of Liberals was found in a broadcast by Mr. Louw. Asked what were the main grievances of the African in the urban areas, he replied: "He has no grievances. He has had some in the past, over housing and so on, but these are being overcome." Asked, "Why does he believe he has a grievance?" Mr. Louw declared, "He has been told he has one."

Mr. Louw, who considered men like Alan Paton "a bunch of sentimentalists", probably would consider treasonable the Liberal Party program "that no person be debarred from participating in the Government and other democratic process of the country by reason only of race, colour or creed." In the embittered mind of Eric Louw, Liberalism, Communism, Christian missionaries, the British Colonial Office, Jewish Capitalism, the Vatican, the United States, the United Nations, and Pandit Nehru are all embroiled in conspiring against South Africa's "white civilization".

When he spoke in Parliament of my arrest, the External Affairs Minister had his innings with the material—notes, messages, and duplicates of despatches—that the Special Branch seized from me. It was not one of his better efforts at character assassination. There was no mention of the results of the "questioning" that was the excuse for my detention. At one stage, he swung the attack to the Canadian Press and the *Toronto Star,* complaining that his reply to Canadian protest cables had not been circulated by the Canadian Press or printed by the *Toronto Star.* This was untrue; Mr. Louw's reply had been printed.

Skilfully extracting the words from their context, Mr. Louw endeavoured to prove that I had been instructed to write a series of articles dealing mainly with violence. (The actual message suggested one magazine article "mainly violence anecdotes; second article Apartheid explanation".) He also managed to overlook the specific order, "Want views on both sides on aims and likelihood of achieving them."

A good example of the Louw technique came when he purported to read from my reference to Governor-General Swart having once entered Parliament brandishing a whip. Under Mr. Louw's skilled editing, the word "usually" was inserted to make it read that Swart "usually entered Parliament".

Mr. Louw went on for four hours in this fashion, managing to include in his attack the British, American, and Swedish press and the British Broadcasting Corporation, all of us guilty of "distorting" racial events and policies in South Africa. However, the honours of the day went to the Opposition. Harry Lawrence, a Progressive Party M.P. and formerly Minister of Justice under Gen. Smuts, began by saying he did not want to defend or condemn me, but he wanted to object to the way the Government had acted.

"As a result of the action the Government took in this case," Mr. Lawrence said, "Phillips is now writing articles millions of people are reading, describing how he spent three gloomy days in a South African jail for writing and reporting the truth about South Africa." As he spoke, there was silence all around him, from the Nationalist ministers facing him and from the Opposition benches.

My arrest had been a blunder, and by then even the Government realized it. Assuming that they had wanted to make an example of a foreign correspondent and frighten their contacts, why had they picked on a Canadian? Canada was one of South Africa's few remaining friends—or if friends is too strong a word, non-enemies. From voting against South Africa at the United Nations in 1958, we had modified our position to abstaining from voting against her Apartheid policies in the 1959 General Assembly.

Why did the Nationalist Government throw all this goodwill away by jailing a Canadian newspaperman in a common prison under a law that denied its victims the fundamental rights of habeas corpus, of legal counsel, and of knowing the charge against them?

Only in Apartheid Land could such folly become government policy. There everything is topsy turvy; and the Nationalists, who live in daily fear of being swamped by the African masses, by their own blind actions hasten the day of reckoning. This will be the racialists' epitaph, that in trying to curb black nationalism by force, they sped the growth of what they feared most.

18. CONCLUSION

DURBAN JAIL was uneasy on the evening of Saturday, April 9. There was a stiffening of discipline, the warders officiously trying to stifle the spread of cell-to-cell rumours. Staff radios were disconnected and all newspapers in the prison meticulously shredded into unreadability. Despite all these precautions on top of our normal isolation, we political prisoners learned, within a few hours of the event, that an attempt had been made on the life of Prime Minister Verwoerd.

Had the would-be assassin been an African, there would have been a blood bath not only throughout the country but in the jail itself that night. However, the shots had been fired by a wealthy English farmer, David Pratt, and there were no recriminations. Instead, all the country's factions were briefly united by shock and revulsion and the most significant result of the shooting was that the victim, Dr. Verwoerd, emerged stronger than ever in his hold over the Nationalist Party and the Apartheid State.

Talk of coalition ceased. This had been the Opposition United Party aim, but they had forfeited all respect by voting with the Government to introduce the Emergency Regulations and ban the African political congresses. The United Party had nothing to offer the Nationalists and Dr. Verwoerd didn't need them. The majority of white South Africans remained committed to white supremacy and opposed to even the mildest consultation with the Africans.

The Liberal Party leadership was in jail, and without any Members of Parliament the party was blocked effectively from carrying on its struggle for a multi-racial South Africa. The left wing Congress of Democrats, which competed with the Liberals in offering co-operation to non-whites, also found its leaders jailed.

The only functioning opposition group was the Progressive Party, with its twelve members in the House of Assembly. Its urgent call for consultation with moderate African leaders was echoed by Leslie Lulofs, president of the Federated Chamber of Industries, speaking for the wealthy industrialists. Mr. Lulofs went to the Cabinet urging arbitration machinery between the Government and responsible Negro leaders, and offered to introduce those leaders to the Cabinet. Mr. J. H. Moolman, himself a Nationalist, the president of the International Wool Board, suggested that the Government ease African grievances.

These were hopeful portents, but Mr. Lulofs spoke without the support of the influential Chamber of Mines, which was on record as having no intention of protesting against Apartheid. And the industrialists were also handicapped in talking to the Government by the fact that 89 per cent of the country's industry and commerce was in the hands of the English-speaking community.

"You are only interested in profits," Dr. Verwoerd told a deputation of business men a few days before he was wounded. "I am interested in preserving the heritage of our people. I would rather see a poor South Africa that was white than a rich South Africa that was black." No compromise, no concessions. Dr. Verwoerd would administer the mixture as before. There would be more riots; they would be put down with more force.

(Costs of the 1960 emergency began with $140,000 a day to keep the Defence Force partially mobilized, plus the dislocation to business caused by the call-up of a hundred thousand part-time soldiers; on top of this was the estimated $56,000,000 loss in production during the African stay-at-home strikes; and finally the capital loss on securities of nearly $1,400,000,000 between January 1 and May 1.)

With Dr. Verwoerd in hospital, the Cabinet's senior Minister, Paul Sauer, led the Government. Mr. Sauer made a "new deal" speech in which he said: "The old book of South African history was closed at Sharpeville. For the immediate future South Africa will have to reconsider in earnest and with honesty her whole approach to the native question. We must create a new spirit which must restore overseas faith, both white and non-white, in South Africa."

Mr. Sauer said the reference book system, or pass laws, would have to be revised and "healthy contacts" established between the black residents and the white authorities in the urban townships.

This trial balloon was quickly shot down by Eric Louw, who reminded Mr. Sauer that only the Prime Minister himself had the right to make policy declarations. And the diehard De Wet Nel, Minister for Bantu Affairs, brought word from the Prime Minister's sickbed: "Dr. Verwoerd believes more than ever now that the policy being followed in South Africa is the correct one."

Mr. Nel, who recently forbade civil servants to use the salutation "Dear Sir" when writing to Africans, was joined by Mr. Willie Maree, Minister of Bantu Education, and author of an order banning shaking hands with Africans. ("Africans," he declared, "persist in trying to shake hands; but it is only those who are trying to become Westernized, and that's what we're trying to prevent." Africans, of course, shook hands long before they first met white men.)

According to Willie Maree, the Government would not be forced, either by a handful of terrorists or the decisions of the outside world, to make concessions. Apartheid would be intensified, and the only possible solution was to spend millions of pounds on Bantustans. "We must do in ten years," he said, "what we expected to do in fifty years. For my part I do not care what it costs. We must do it in the interests of our own safety and for peace and order."

Development of the reserves that form Bantustans cost the Government about $30,000,000 in the first ten years. Nationalists boast about this expenditure but overlook the conclusion of the Government Tomlinson Commission that in the first ten years development of the Bantu homelands required $292,320,000. In other words, only about one-tenth as much money has been invested in this program as was needed, and the vaunted 1960 allocation of $10,000,000 still fell far short of what was needed to help the reserves in a losing battle against hunger and poverty.

The professed goal of the Nationalist extremists was that the more than three million Africans scratching a living from the reserves would be joined by another three million Negroes who now till the white man's farms, and the nearly three million who live in urban areas. In Bantustan all Africans would be allowed to develop. Indeed Apartheid is now even a dirty word among Nationalists, and they are substituting "Separate Development" or "Separate Freedom" in an effort to deodorize this repugnant and unworkable policy.

The Government still believed after Sharpeville that good public relations could convince the outside world that they were not unfair to the African, and by publicizing the expenditure of $10,000,000 a year on the development of Bantustans could change world opinion that South Africa is an international "polecat"—as the Nationalist newspaper *Die Burger* put it—and at the same time restore stability inside the country.

Justice Minister Frans Erasmus warned white South Africans to prepare for the day when cheap African labour would no longer be so readily available, when they would have to make personal sacrifices in adapting themselves to that situation. The initial test would be in higher taxes to find money for Bantustan, and the white South African was told that he had only one choice—financing Apartheid or abdicating to black domination.

Everything was delightfully simple in the mind of the Apartheidists. The disturbances were the result of Communist agitation and African gangsters. Millions of Africans were happy and contented and actively supporting the Government. They had no grievances.

South Africa suffered a strange form of schizophrenia, a split personality that permitted politicians to make these statements while their civil servants, social workers, economists, and statisticians produced a flow of contradictory evidence. No grievances among the Africans? What about the coal miners at Coalbrook? According to the Government's chief inspector of mines, W. T. Dalling, there were Africans at Coalbrook working underground seven days a week for twelve hours a day, and payments were irregular.

Will the Coalbrook miners be packed off to the Bantustan native reserve and their places taken by the advocates of white supremacy? Not likely.

No grievances when ten thousand African children die each year from gastro-enteritis? When 95 per cent of the Africans living in Durban's Cato Manor slum exist below the subsistence level? When at Johannesburg some gold mines make $2,800,000 a month profit, and only 30 per cent of the Africans earn enough for a bare minimum standard of living?

The racialists' facile explanation that the African protests were the result of intimidation by gangsters falls apart when the march of Philip Kgosana and thirty thousand men and women from Langa and Nyanga is considered. This was no gangster demonstration; the gangster element only came to the fore after the police rounded up moderate African leaders.

Prosperous African underground figures tried to bring together the remnants of the African National Congress and Pan-Africanist Congress leadership. The one-day strike call on April 24 fizzled badly, suggesting that the new black underground needed further organization. Nor was it certain that the two congresses could sink their differences. Robert Sobukwe's Pan-Africanists strengthened their position, but more at the expense of Chief Luthuli and the A.N.C. than by converting new followers. And the combined membership of the two congresses was less than a hundred thousand, in an African population nearing ten million.

Literally beaten into submission, their locations patrolled by armoured cars and riddled with informers, the politically minded Africans needed time to find new leaders. Whether they would stick to non-violent methods or, as Japie Basson warned, turn South Africa into a new Cyprus or Algeria, could not be foreseen. It was quite possible that a new and reckless movement might emerge before the year was out.

As the Nationalists announced their intention to speed up and clean up Apartheid, a significant document made its appearance in South Africa. "What does need stressing," it began, "is that it is not a sufficient answer to Apartheid to reveal the enormous human suffering, the deep inroads on human dignity, the economic fatuity and wastefulness.... There is only one remedy, and that is to offer a constructive alternative that is better than Apartheid."

These were the words not of any radical group but of Denis Cowen, Professor of Comparative Law in the University of Cape Town. Moreover, they appeared under the sponsorship of the Anglo-American Corporation of South Africa, in a magazine published "in the interests of mining and industrial progress".

"Each year," said Prof. Cowen, "Apartheid brings additional burdens and frustrations and makes the risk of eventual retaliations greater. Its implementation carries with it its own inherent and grave dangers of economic impoverishment and social turmoil—and the fear of these may yet come to weigh as heavily as the fears which give life to Apartheid itself."

Prof. Cowen suggested a non-racial democracy as the only alternative to Apartheid. He did not advocate the immediate introduction of universal adult franchise, but recommended that if a qualified franchise were adopted, the qualifications should be devised to give a really substantial number of non-whites an effective voice in the government.

"The need for the whites," said Prof. Cowen, "was not to get themselves into a position where all possibility of gradualism is swept aside in racial passion."

Sponsorship by the Anglo-American Corporation may have been the kiss of death for Prof. Cowen's rational proposals. The Nationalist Party for years has accused the United Party of being in the pocket of big business, and this bogey has been a successful vote-winner.

More likely to succeed in the struggle against Apartheid was Archbishop Joost de Blank's campaign to put pressure on the Dutch Reformed Church. "If the church is to have any chance of survival in this country," said Dr. de Blank, "the Africans must be shown by constructive action and not by words alone that the churches have turned their backs on compulsory Apartheid once and for all.

"After Sharpeville, almost every church issued a statement clearly condemning policies that could lead to such a shocking state of affairs, and calling for active co-operation between the races. But until the Dutch Reformed Churches identify themselves with this repudiation, the Christian faith is unable to make much progress and is in urgent danger of complete rejection by the African people."

Backed by the Archbishop of Canterbury, who called on the South African Government to drop Apartheid and hold "peace talks" with Chief Luthuli, Dr. de Blank took the strong line of threatening to ostracize the Dutch Reformed Churches unless they repudiated Apartheid. The hope on this front came from the dozen dominies of the Dutch Reformed Churches who secretly approached Japie Basson and expressed their second thoughts concerning the spiritual justification for Apartheid. If a majority of dominies would adopt this view, the official stand of the Dutch Reformed Churches in favour of Apartheid could be reversed; and this would have immediate effect on the Government and its supporters, most of whom are devout church-goers.

Another pressure movement was the consumer boycott of South African exports. This was not a success in itself, nor did it promise to be an effective weapon. The Union's major exports are gold, then wool; the market for gold is assured, but that for wool is vulnerable. Russia is a major buyer of South African wool, and China recently entered the market on a large scale. This explains the plea of Wool Board Chairman Moolman, asking the Government to moderate its racial policies. A boycott by wool buyers on the wholesale level would have an immediate impact on the very farmers who back the Nationalists.

The danger of an effective boycott was that it might knit the racialists closer inside the white man's laager, and an out-and-out dictatorship might result. Another argument was that boycotts would hurt Africans more than whites; but the present suffering of the black people was a sufficient reply to this. Most of them knew the saturation point in suffering, and would gladly bear up under one more burden if it showed promise of easing their way of life.

Persuasion was tried at the Commonwealth Prime Ministers Conference. It failed miserably, almost contemptuously rejected by Eric Louw. The next logical step for the Commonwealth was to impose some form of sanctions; the next logical move from the world at large, action at the United Nations to deprive South Africa of its mandate over the former German colony of South West Africa.

More likely than any of these moves to force the Nationalists into retreat was an accelerated disintegration of race relations. Obdurate and unyielding, Prime Minister Verwoerd and his closest supporters were capable of bringing down the entire nation into chaos. Their blind indifference to the economic and political consequences of Apartheid could only promote violence.

Sharpeville, Langa, and Nyanga did not signal the D-day for an African uprising. The black people of South Africa were not so revolutionary as their brothers to the north, nor did they have the education or organization for effective political action. The process of self-education gained pace under the police whips, and there were teachers in Ghana, Algeria, Egypt, and Guinea ready to instruct the Africans in the latest techniques of guerrilla warfare. If the 1960 disturbances were not the D-day, they were the Africans' Dieppe raid.

The casualties included eighteen thousand Africans arrested within eight weeks after the Sharpeville massacre. Among these were about fifteen hundred African, Indian, and Coloured leaders held indefinitely under the Emergency Regulations. The others were "agitators" and "intimidators" accused by the police of being in the urban areas without the necessary passes. Normally, these passless persons would have been shunted back to the reserves, but the racialists now found themselves with a problem. Trouble was brewing on the reserves; white storekeepers lived in fear and government-appointed chiefs and headmen ruled uneasily. Could the Government take the risk of dumping these semi-sophisticated city "agitators" amongst the already stirring tribal Africans?

The alternative was concentration camps. And when I was expelled from South Africa as its autumn began, the police state was very close to entering its concentration-camp stage.

Nor would this save the tragic country from another racial explosion within a matter of months. Even Dr. Verwoerd agreed on that.

QC

I